BROTHERS
IN BLACK

JAMIE WALL

BROTHERS IN BLACK

The long history of brotherhood in New Zealand rugby

ALLEN&UNWIN
SYDNEY•MELBOURNE•AUCKLAND•LONDON

First published in 2019

Text © Jamie Wall 2019

Allen & Unwin
Level 3, 228 Queen Street
Auckland 1010, New Zealand
Phone: (64 9) 377 3800
Email: info@allenandunwin.com
Web: www.allenandunwin.co.nz

83 Alexander Street
Crows Nest NSW 2065, Australia
Phone: (61 2) 8425 0100

A catalogue record for this book is available from
the National Library of New Zealand.

ISBN 978 1 98854 717 6

Design by Kate Barraclough
Set in Adobe Caslon Pro
Printed and bound in Australia by Griffin Press, part of Ovato

10 9 8 7 6 5 4 3 2 1

The paper in this book is FSC® certified.
FSC® promotes environmentally responsible,
socially beneficial and economically viable
management of the world's forests.

FOR PAUL H

CONTENTS

INTRODUCTION

'BROTHERS ON THREE! ONE-TWO-THREE BROTHERS!' That was part of the ritual at our home of Kilbirnie Park, or wherever we ended up playing on Wellington's numerous club rugby fields. Many were, and probably still are, of dubious quality. Most of us were never going to play in a higher grade. Some, like me, spent a good chunk of our time watching from the sidelines with water bottles or linesmen's flags in our hands. But it never stopped our Senior 1sts, and every other team from Poneke FC (a club so ancient it's older than the convention of calling it 'rugby'), sounding out that call before a game, at half-time, at full-time, and at the end of every training. On every park, in every changing room where the paint is peeling from the walls, on every freezing night under lights in the driving rain.

It becomes ingrained in you. This idea that rugby is indeed a brotherhood, that you've got this feeling of belonging that no one else can understand. You and your teammates all go through something together, strive to achieve the same goal for 80 minutes, sweat, bleed and fight until you walk off, bonded.

Of course, if you've ever read anything about rugby at any level of the game, none of this will be new. It's not even unique to rugby—you'll find it in pretty much every other team sport or social pursuit. We all aspire to belong to something, which is why we invoked that fraternal phrasing so often. We're all brothers out there, because to think of it that way makes us play better, because we're playing for each other.

But what about the ones who have felt that way since birth? The literal brothers who step out onto the field alongside one another, bringing the genetic connection, the shared skills, the deepened knowledge. It's hard to imagine playing rugby as a kid and not playing in a team with some sort of brotherly connection. It's essentially impossible to be in a rugby club that doesn't have one.

We're all brothers out there, because to think of it that way makes us play better, because we're playing for each other.

The vast majority will play out their careers without any fanfare. Some may end up on an honours board, or in a club blazer. Every now and then one will hit the big time. Then there are those brothers who make it together, who go all the way. To the holy grail of rugby: an All Blacks jersey.

Brothers have been part of the All Blacks since the beginning. Through both world wars, when the game itself went through a gigantic upheaval. Through the amateur era of punch-ups and mud, to the big money- and media-driven world we live in today. One thing is for certain: they have played a part in almost every single notable event in the team's history.

There were brothers on the Invincibles tour. Brothers in the 1956 first-ever series win over the Springboks. Twin brothers on the field when the All Blacks first won the World Cup in 1987. Brothers among the first names listed for the series win in South

Africa in 1996. Brothers in the side that won the World Cup final in 2011 (one out on Eden Park and one on the bench). A try-scorer in the 2015 final would later become one of the first trio of brothers to take the field together for the All Blacks.

Across history, it's a story that is told and retold. Some of the names here will be familiar, like Clarke and Meads, Savea and Barrett. Some might not be, unless you're old enough to remember them or are a bit of a rugby historian. To see the team's history through their experience is to be granted a unique look at the most powerful force in world sport.

They are the Brothers in Black. This is their story.

The 1883 Auckland representative
team photo features a 21-year-old
Joe Warbrick right in the middle,
draping his arms around the player
in front. **NEW ZEALAND RUGBY MUSEUM**

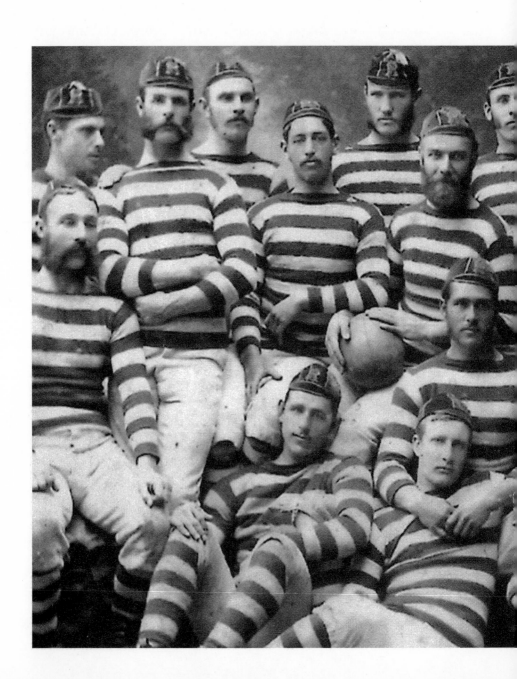

THE WARBRICKS AND WYNYARDS

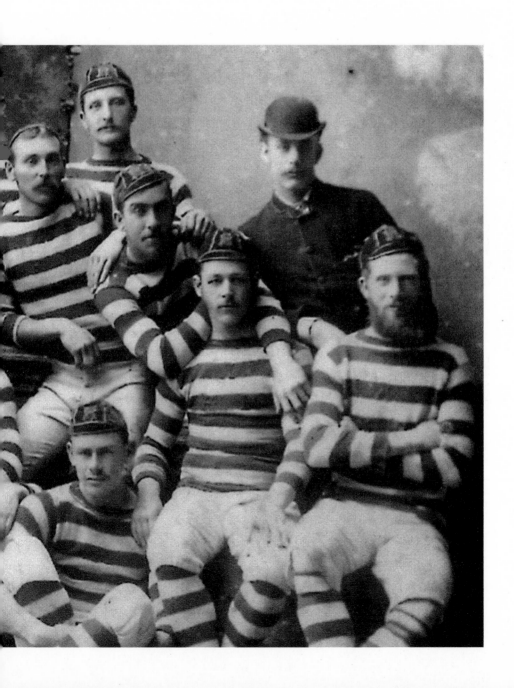

THIRTEEN MONTHS AWAY FROM HOME. One hundred and seven matches. A tour that laid the foundations of test rugby, put together by one of five brothers from the Bay of Plenty and bolstered by another three from Auckland. If rugby truly is New Zealand's religion, then this is the chapter of Genesis, and the Warbrick and Wynyard brothers are its prophets.

If you're not religious, here's a more scientific way of explaining just how long ago this story takes place. You can look at the history of the game in at least three distinct eras. There is the time we have now, the modern age in which every single drop of sweat that drips from the players' brows is caught in slow motion as it falls onto their scientifically designed and sponsor-laden jerseys. There was the amateur age, in which sleeves were longer, boots and rucks actually got dirty, and the compensation for sacrificing your body and time for an All Blacks jersey was some free beers and a pat on the back.

But while that amateur era is what everyone gets all misty-eyed and somewhat hypocritically nostalgic over, there was an even earlier time in which rugby in New Zealand evolved from the ether. The primordial ooze. A Cambrian Explosion as opposed to the amateur age's Cretaceous Period that ended with the dinosaurs who had ruled the game for so long finally dying out.

The story of Joseph, Frederick, William, Alfred and Arthur

Warbrick and George, Henry and William Wynyard is the prehistory of the All Blacks. They played in a New Zealand representative side that existed long before the team known as 'The Originals' made the All Blacks name famous, and generations before the game was used by players as a way of making money. Because there's the twist in this one: that's exactly why the Warbricks, Wynyards and the rest of the 1888–89 New Zealand Natives set out for their epic tour of Great Britain. It was a revenue-gathering exercise, in a time when the laws around amateurism were still being dreamed up and fought about in London gentlemen's clubs. They were the pioneers of an age when New Zealand, and indeed the rest of the world, was barely recognisable compared to what exists today.

To set the scene, this was a country in which Māori and Pākehā had only recently finished fighting an actual war for control of large parts of the North Island. Auckland's population was 130,000, and infant mortality was outrageously high. So it's a minor miracle that the five Warbrick brothers even made it to school age. They were born between 1860 and 1868 in Rotorua, with their father, Abraham, an English immigrant and mother, Nga Karauna Paerau, of Ngāti Rangitihi descent.

Joe Warbrick was a forward-thinking man with a plan by the time he'd finished at St Stephen's Native School in what is now South Auckland. While he was still a young teenager he took the opportunity to play senior club rugby for the Ponsonby club up the line in the city. This was, of course, in the late nineteenth century, so the game of rugby barely resembled what it is now.

Games revolved around mostly dribbling the ball up and down the field by opposing forward packs, who would hack at each other's shins when they got an opportunity. Rules and team numbers varied depending on where you were playing the game, and scoring points was done mostly by kicking the ball through the goalposts. It's hard to get an exact feel for what it would have been like on the field of play back then but, for anyone watching, it probably looked like a bunch of dogs fighting over a bone.

Joe was picked for the Auckland representative side aged only 15, which makes him maybe the youngest first-class player in New Zealand rugby history ('maybe', because records of the time are pretty sketchy). He moved to Wellington in 1879 and played for them as well, then alternated between Auckland and Hawke's Bay until 1887. In 1884, he was picked as one of New Zealand's first-ever rugby representatives for a tour to the colonies of New South Wales and Queensland. The team won all eight of the games played, with Jack Taiaroa and Joe becoming the first Māori to represent New Zealand at any sport. They wore the colours of the union that had organised the tour, Otago. The woollen pullovers, which would have been extremely uncomfortable to wear in the hot Australian sun, were dark blue with a gold fern.

For anyone watching, it probably looked like a bunch of dogs fighting over a bone.

Meanwhile, the three Wynyard brothers of Ngāti Hikairo heritage had established their playing careers with the North Shore club in Devonport. William, more commonly known as 'Tabby', was definitely the more accomplished of the brothers, having played for Auckland before moving south and setting up at the Poneke club in Wellington. Like Tabby, the other two had nicknames for easier identification: George was known as 'Sherry' and Henry as 'Pie'. It's been lost to history as to whether that was due to what George liked to drink and Henry's weight, and who knows why William was called Tabby.

The short hop over to what is now Australia planted a seed in Joe Warbrick's mind. Why not go further, play longer? Head to where the game began and show them not only the strength of the game in New Zealand, but also a glimpse of this new colony's culture—and charge people for the experience.

It wasn't a particularly new idea; cricket had pioneered the convention of touring in the decades beforehand. English cricket teams had been to North America and Australia in the late 1850s and early 1860s. Most notably in the context of this story, an Australian Aboriginal cricket team had travelled to England in 1868 to play 47 matches.

In the same year as the Natives were to leave, a privately organised British Isles tour came Down Under, which was to be the forerunner of the massive cash-cow these days known as the British & Irish Lions. The tourists had managed to win 27 games, lost only two and somehow drawn six across Australia and New Zealand, and had done so after having their captain drown in a boating accident halfway through.

Plans were set in motion for a much longer expedition in reverse. It was a ground-breaking move, and Joe would employ only slightly more than the bare minimum of players needed to field a team. The good news was all four of his brothers pretty much fitted the bill for the tourists, so that was five out of the way.

'Pretty much', as in Alfred (Alf) was 28 at the time of the tour, and his rugby prowess wasn't exactly noted. Neither was Arthur's, who was 25. The younger boys, William (Billy) and Fred, were closest to Joe's level of talent for the game, and that would prove to be rather important as the tour progressed. Tabby and Pie Wynyard were also chosen, with Sherry a later addition to the touring squad. Like the older Warbrick brothers, Pie and Sherry weren't known as the best players, but right now the squad needed jersey-fillers.

That was because, in the lead-up to the tour, finding players that would commit to a year's absence from their homes was proving a bit more difficult than Joe Warbrick had originally thought. He enlisted the help of Thomas Eyton, a veteran of the Land Wars, to be the tour promoter. Also included was a young visionary from Wellington, Thomas Ellison. Eyton and Ellison's involvement and subsequent written accounts of the tour have proved invaluable to historians in the years since, with Ellison going into detail about the matches in his pioneering coaching manual, *The Art of Rugby Football*.

It was Ellison who suggested that the Natives wear a uniform that would represent all New Zealand this time. The jersey would be black, with a silver fern.

Joe had originally envisaged the tour to be a Māori side, and that the cultural intrigue generated in the British Isles would mean that crowds would be showing up to see more than just rugby games. That wasn't to be the case due to the lack of availability of enough Māori players, so numbers had to be made up with five Pākehā players to bring the full squad up to 26 (which would be the bare minimum the All Blacks would take to one single test match these days). It also meant the team's name had to be changed from the 'New Zealand Maori' to 'New Zealand Natives'.

Then there was the issue of money and how the team could circumvent the amateur status of the game. It's a safe bet that most who were interested in being involved in the tour saw it as a business venture first and foremost, and it would rely heavily on the 60 per cent of gate takings the promoters would keep from each game. That's the reason the tour ended up with its iconic, never-to-be-repeated length.

The team assembled and played a series of warm-up games around the country. Unfortunately for Joe, he suffered a serious foot injury in a game against Auckland, which would hinder his involvement in the tour thereafter.

The team stepped off their ship in London on 27 September 1888. It was an auspicious time to arrive in what was then essentially the capital of the world, three days before the fourth in an ongoing spate of grisly murders in the city's East End, committed by someone the press was already dubbing Jack the Ripper. Queen Victoria's reign was at its absolute peak, and the British Empire stretched from all the way down to New Zealand, across India, to large tracts of Africa and the top half of North America. These were heady times, the sort that you're reminded of to a grand degree as you wander through the streets of London today, where the edifices of the men who built the empire stand tall over the traffic and bustle. Mutton-chops and bowler hats would have been a constant sight for the Natives as they made their way south of London to Surrey, where they had their first game on British soil against Richmond. The sight of them was an impressive one for *The Daily Telegraph*, which remarked:

> We have been invaded, and the Maori is upon us. Full five-and-twenty strong he landed . . . busily preparing and practising for the forthcoming fifty or sixty pitched battles to be fought in the course of the coming season. Yet the timid may take heart of grace; this invasion of peaceful and

pleasant character threatens no new danger to England. It is one of those ever-welcome colonial invasions in which our fellow subjects from across the sea come to wage friendly war with us in some of our national sports and pastimes.

Seems fairly friendly, a far cry from the sort of nonsense that gets flung about whenever the All Blacks play in the UK these days. Although it was followed up by a comment straight out of the nineteenth century: 'The Maoris have certainly progressed since Captain James Cook found the finely painted and neatly tattooed ancestors of our visitors eating each other out in the bush.'

With that charming bit of colonial-era racial theory still fresh on the broadsheet, the team lined up for their first game. Their opponents, Richmond, were a thrown-together bunch and got duly dispatched 4–1 (tries were worth one point and shots at goal, two). It was the first of 52 scheduled games around England and Wales. That number was to increase, however, as would the realities of undertaking such a huge tour. By the time the team recorded its fifth game, injuries were starting to mount up, with Billy Warbrick among the worst affected with a broken collarbone.

This wasn't a situation where they could simply call on replacements, either. In their game against Moseley, they lost four players in one match. Another hurdle for the tourists to overcome was the generous hospitality laid on for them by the aristocratic benefactors of the game in southern England. Free booze wasn't exactly the best preparation for games, such as at the fixture in Middlesex, where the Earl of Sheffield shouted them lunch and a plentiful amount of champagne on game day. It's not at all surprising that the Natives ended up losing 9–0 and two players were found asleep before the official pre-match team photo.

However, things were about to change when the team headed north. Yorkshire and Lancashire were, at the time, the UK's strongest rugby-playing regions, so this was to be an exceptionally tough leg. Billy Warbrick returned to the action in the game against Northumberland County after only three weeks out with his injury, and Joe made his debut in the game the following week after recovering from his foot complaint. Sherry Wynyard joined his brothers in the team at around this time, having been in the UK in search of work.

The Natives' backs chucked on some rain jackets and continued the game dressed as if they were heading out for dinner.

Against Carlisle, the Natives had a match that was very much in the farcical spirit of their pre-match piss-up in Middlesex, if not anywhere near as fun. By now it was late November, and the weather had taken a decided turn for the worse. The game, which was being dominated by the visitors, had to resume after half-time minus three of the home side. They'd decided it was too cold and packed it in. Maybe it was the good old colonial spirit, but the Natives' backs chucked on some rain jackets and continued the game dressed as if they were heading out for dinner.

By now, it was becoming clear that some members of the touring party were far more useful than others. While a number racked up appearances week in, week out, Alf Warbrick was proving to be a non-starter, as was Joe, who seemed to be permanently injured and was also preoccupied with the running of the tour. Compounding their problems was the increasingly brutal schedule, which increased from the original 52 matches to a massive 74 in the UK.

At the time, the game of rugby was rough at best and lethal at the very worst. Deaths weren't uncommon; in the four years following the tour, the RFU recorded 78 fatalities at all levels of the game. However, considering their heavy workload and lack of modern medical arrangements (such as a team doctor, and knowledge of warm-up and cool-down exercises), and the use of hard liquor for any sort of pain relief, the Natives' record by the time they crossed the Irish Sea to play their first international match was still impressively high.

The spirits in the touring party, though, were not. There were talks of a mutiny due to the arduous nature of what the tour had become. But the tour promoters held all the revenue, so not fulfilling their commitments simply wasn't an option as mutinous players wouldn't have any way of returning home.

So it's quite remarkable the New Zealand Natives team comprehensively thrashed Ireland in their test match in Dublin. The score was 13–4; four goals and a try versus a goal and a try to the home side. By now, Fred Warbrick was establishing himself as one of the stars of the team, and played a leading hand in the Natives' dominant performance. The youngest of the brothers, he played as a halfback on the tour. Billy Warbrick was in the side that beat Ireland as well.

The team's next big match was in Swansea, against the side whose later fixture against the 1905 New Zealand team would go down as the veritable beginning of the Common Era for the All Blacks. Like their future counterparts, the Natives went down to the Welsh in front of a packed crowd, although in far less controversial circumstances. They were fairly beaten 5–0, and the only dodgy thing was that by the time the game was over, the lack of light meant that it was hard for the crowd on one side of the field to make out what was happening on the other. This was due to the fact that the UK was deep into winter.

By now, they were about halfway through the tour, which had seen more than a few of the 20 additional fixtures played. The next test would be against England at Blackheath in London, and this was to be the game that would stick in the memory as the one where the visitors got shafted.

The infamous loss to Wales in 1905 can be pinned down to a possibly understandable lapse by the referee. In that instance, a try scored by Bob Deans that might have won the game for the All Blacks was disallowed because the man in charge, John Dallas, wasn't wearing boots and couldn't keep up with the play. The 7–0 loss to England that the Natives suffered in 1889, though, seems far more likely to have been due to a concerted effort by referee (and later Sir) George Rowland Hill to help the home team win for the entire length of the game.

Instead of a try being disallowed, two contentious tries were given. Billy Warbrick allegedly grounded the ball in his own in-goal area after a kick went through, yet Hill awarded a try to the English player who followed up and 'scored'. This happened again later in the first half, except this time it was Harry Lee who had forced the ball dead for the Natives.

Worse, and more farcical, circumstances were yet to come. English captain Andrew Stoddart dropped the ball after his shorts were ripped off, leading the Natives side to halt, presuming he'd restore his dignity by fetching another pair. Unfortunately, another English player took the opportunity to run away and score under the sticks to settle the result, which led to three of the Natives players leaving the field in protest.

Needless to say, feelings between the two sides weren't great by full-time. Just to rub it in, the RFU demanded two apologies from the team for the walk-off, and treated the Natives as unwelcome guests for the remainder of the tour.

English captain Andrew Stoddart dropped the ball after his shorts were ripped off, leading the Natives side to halt, presuming he'd restore his dignity by fetching another pair.

There it was: an unhappy start to an often unhappy history of Anglo–New Zealand rugby relations. It also hadn't helped that the reaction from the English authorities and press to the Natives' pre-match ceremonial haka showed a complete lack of understanding (another thing that hasn't changed to the present day). One administrator saw it as 'an advertising spectacle', while the *Sporting Life* described it as 'a whoop in the vernacular which caused great amusement'.

While tours in later years would finish after a big test match, the Natives still had a punishing schedule of matches throughout the north of England to complete before they could board a ship for the long voyage home. This was, though, the area of the country where the New Zealanders definitely felt the most at home, because of the massive disparity between the sort of people that played the game there compared with the south.

Joe Warbrick himself had this to say in a post-tour interview with *The Press* about the attitude of the landed gentry who watched the game in the south:

As long as the Native team were losing they were jolly good fellows in the eyes of the crowd. But as soon as they commenced to win they were hooted and the papers were full of the weakness of the home side and the rough play of the visitors.

Greg Ryan's account of the tour, *Forerunners of the All Blacks*, describes the climate of the game in England at the time as having a limited lifespan. While the RFU's blatant class-based hypocrisy and adherence to amateurism was scorned, the relative egalitarianism of the game in the north was a jarring contrast:

> These people were untouched by public-school traditions. Even the wealthiest northern rugby administrators had close contacts with working-class players. Although some of them had accumulated enough money to be considered part of the upper middle class, they were snubbed by its 'gentlemen' who viewed hard-earned industrial wealth with a degree of contempt. More so than in the south, the northern elite maintained links with their local communities and with their working-class origins.
>
> A working-class game also meant greater tolerance of hard or rough play. Unlike gentlemen, and those in the professions, miners and factory workers were used to taking physical knocks as part of their daily routine. Taking them on the field was no different.

Given that the Natives side was full of working men as well, it's not hard to see why the reception from clubs in the north— and the officiating of games in that region—was described as far more fair in players' later accounts of the tour.

The team left the UK with a respectable record of 49 wins, 20 losses and five draws. However, it's important to point out that while the team deserves all the credit in the world for taking on such a huge number of games in a comparatively short space of time, they weren't quite the on-field phenomenon that the All Blacks would become in later years. The rugby they played was simple but effective, which was a bit of a downer to locals who had flocked to see these men from the bottom of the earth. As recorded by *The Daily Telegraph*:

> The curious ones in the crowd . . . who expected some form of unconventional 'new departure' were disappointed. They play a fairly orthodox rugby game, but nothing out of the common . . . Suffice it to record that the New Zealanders have learnt and preserved every rule and tradition of the game.

One feat the Natives can claim as wholly their own is that they remain the only New Zealand representative side to take on a fair representation of the strength of English and Welsh rugby. This was, of course, only six years away from the northern clubs banding together and splitting from their southern counterparts to form what we now know as rugby league, an event that severely restricted the talent pool that either country could draw from.

While the Natives' tour is mostly remembered for its trailblazing path across the United Kingdom, it was far from over by the time they headed back to the southern hemisphere. There was still a scheduled 16-game stopover in Australia and then a further 17 games upon their return to New Zealand.

Tragedy struck while the team was on their second-to-last leg, in Australia. Wi Karauria, who had played 32 games in a row in the UK before being stricken with tuberculosis, was sent home, where he passed away. There was to be controversy, too, when the team played their second of two matches against Queensland, after the first had ended in a 22–0 drubbing by the visitors.

Some members of the Natives side had been bribed by local bookies to go easy on the Queenslanders and miss a few tackles. When it became apparent in the first half that something was amiss, Joe had a few strong words with his teammates, threatening to expose the players responsible. Whatever he said, it worked, and the team went on to win 11–7. Four players did end up getting shamed and banned from playing anyway—including Arthur Warbrick.

The side made it back to New Zealand, and started the final leg of its tour in Dunedin. Members of the team dropped away as it moved northward to finally finish by playing Auckland. The tour had lasted over a year. Their achievements on the field, however, would be eclipsed by the influence that the tour would have off it.

The local unions were exceptionally wary of what had transpired over the past year. For all the modern talk of rugby's position as a game for all people in New Zealand, it was still run by a set of gentlemen who saw themselves as an extension of the powers-that-be back in England. Their role, as they saw it, was to safeguard the amateur traditions of the game at all costs. Therefore, no more privately organised tours would be allowed to take place unless they were run by a supreme governing body. The Natives had forced the formation of what would become the New Zealand Rugby Football Union, whose first act was to sanction a team to represent the country that would eventually become known as the All Blacks.

The Warbrick brothers had all played a part in the team's record—although some far more than others. While Joe had played a huge role in organising the tour and gathering the men who would play, his on-field contribution was relatively minimal. He played in only 21 games of the entire tour, and almost a quarter of those were played back in New Zealand. However, that's a better return than his older brother Alf, who only managed 16 games, including just four in the UK. While Joe was hampered by injury and the stress of organising the tour, it's clear that Alf just wasn't that good a player. The insistence of the Natives to play as strong a team as possible at all times is the reason why he essentially ended up watching his brothers and mates play footy for a year.

Billy, Fred and Arthur put in good shifts with 59, 65 and 67 games respectively. Out of all the brothers, Billy was generally regarded as the most talented player. He was described by tour promoter Eyton as 'a dashing player, grand tackler, first-class kick, very good at following up, and beyond being occasionally too venturesome, he left nothing to be desired in his play'.

This wasn't the end of his rugby career, either, as he went on to represent Auckland. He and Fred liked what they'd experienced in Queensland and moved there in 1890. They continued to play and represented Queensland against the first official New Zealand team that toured in 1893. As was shockingly common in those days, Billy died young—in 1901, aged only 35.

He wasn't alone in going to the grave early. In fact, the next three years would see the Warbrick brothers reduced to only one surviving sibling.

By 1902, Arthur Warbrick was working as a ferryman on the

Ohiwa River, near Opotiki. In September of that year, he was washed out to sea and drowned, aged 34. In tragically similar circumstances, Fred drowned in a boating accident at Woody Point, north of Brisbane, in 1904.

Joe's death is the most well known. After retiring from playing at the conclusion of the tour, he was coaxed back onto the field to play for Auckland in 1894—a full 17 years after his debut as a 15-year-old. Older brother Alf had established himself as the chief government guide in the burgeoning tourism industry in their home town of Rotorua, and Joe had joined him as a guide by the turn of the century.

One of the main attractions of the geothermal region was the Waimangu Geyser. At the time, it was the largest geyser in the world, capable of eruptions of boiling water up to an incredible 460 metres in the air. Unsurprisingly, health and safety measures at the time weren't up to scratch, and when 41-year-old Joe led three tourists to the edge of the Waimangu in 1903, it erupted violently and the group was swept away and died. Alf was left behind as the only surviving Warbrick brother.

Despite the tragedy, Alf continued on in his role as the tour guide for the region for the next three decades. He passed away in 1940, aged 80.

Tabby Wynyard returned to New Zealand and had a distinguished provincial career with Auckland and Wellington. He was eventually picked to play in the first official New Zealand side that toured Australia in 1893, and lined up against Fred and Billy Warbrick in Queensland. He lived out the rest of his life working in the Department of Agriculture in Wellington, and passed away in 1938, aged 71. His brother Pie played for Wellington as well, and was employed at the Petone freezing works before his death in 1921. Not much is known of Sherry's life in the aftermath of the tour, other than that he moved to Sydney in the 1890s.

He has a handsome, timeless face, the sort that you'd see half-grimacing in pain, walking into a rugby club anywhere in the country after a Saturday-afternoon battle.

There are several team photos of the Natives side, with the most iconic being the one that was posed in a bush setting with the team flanked by gigantic Union Jack and United Tribes flags. Looking at a picture of Joe Warbrick today, you could be confused as to exactly when it was taken. He has a handsome, timeless face, the sort that you'd see half-grimacing in pain, walking into a rugby club anywhere in the country after a Saturday-afternoon battle.

Joe's contribution to the history of the game has not been forgotten. In 2009, he was inducted into the World Rugby Hall of Fame, alongside the greatest names that the sport has produced. The same year, a short film was produced that portrayed a somewhat modernised retelling of the pre-match struggles that the Natives faced on tour.

The 1888–89 New Zealand Natives side left one more legacy. Tom Ellison went on to become one of the first Māori to be admitted to the bar, and practised law in Wellington as well as continuing to play and then administrate rugby. Once the NZRFU was formed in 1892, Ellison's proposal that the official national side continue to wear the uniform that the Natives side used on their tour was accepted.

The black jersey with the silver fern was here to stay.

The first-ever New Zealand representative team, including Edward (back row, third from right) and William Millton (middle row, with the ball). Joe Warbrick (front row, centre) features as well.
NEW ZEALAND RUGBY MUSEUM

EARLY DAYS

WHILE THE WARBRICKS AND WYNYARDS get the glory of being the focus of the story about the crazy 1888–89 New Zealand Natives tour, they weren't actually the first siblings to set foot on a rugby field for New Zealand. That honour goes to William and Edward Millton, All Blacks number 7 and 16.

William wasn't just a player, either. Like Joe Warbrick, he was an organiser, managing the first-ever overseas tour by a New Zealand rugby team—to Australia in 1884. Maybe this is where Joe had his idea to stack his side four years later with his brothers, too, because William brought along his younger brother Edward. Both of them played every game of the highly successful tour, in which the team won every game and outscored their opponents 144–12. William has the distinction of being captain in every single game he ever played for New Zealand, and he also was the first player to kick off a trans-Tasman rugby match.

However, William's story took a decidedly Victorian turn after he finished playing. Aged only 29, he died of typhoid. Edward lived on to be 81.

The next set of brothers to play for New Zealand came along in 1893. Both Alan and Hugh Good were picked to tour Australia, but Hugh couldn't take time away from the family farm in Taranaki. Hugh eventually did get one game a year later, but by then Alan had been replaced in the side. Also playing in that

1894 game against New South Wales was fellow Taranaki player Alfred Cooke. His brother Reuben, who was 10 years his junior, ended up playing for New Zealand in 1903—but Alfred never got to see him play. Sadly, he met an untimely end, shot in a hunting accident in 1900. Reuben started what would become a common theme among brothers who have played for the All Blacks, getting himself sent off for fighting in a match against New South Wales.

The instigator of the fight was said to be Archibald (Archie) McMinn, one of five brothers from Manawatu. His brother Francis (Paddy) was picked for the series the next season against the touring British Isles side. However, by this point no brothers had actually been on the field together in an official test match.

It wasn't until 1905 that the All Blacks would be able to boast that feat. However, that late date had more to do with the fact that Australia didn't become an official test-playing nation until 1899, and venturing any further abroad hadn't been attempted since the Natives tour (the Boer War had also played a role in stifling any test programmes, with more than a few players heading off to fight). Yes, that date is right—while the 1905 'Originals' were on a boat across the oceans to play their famous tour in the UK, another New Zealand rep side was selected to play Australia at Tahuna Park in Dunedin.

Southlanders Charles and Edward (Pat) Purdue played in what was effectively a third-string All Blacks side, but it was still strong enough to beat the Wallabies 14–3. Against the odds of the time, both lived long and happy lives thereafter in Invercargill. The captain that day was John (Jack) Spencer, from Wellington. Two years later, his brother George joined him in the All Blacks tour to Australia. However, it's what they did next that separates them from every other set of brothers in this book.

By 1908, rugby league was making its first inroads into Australasia and immediately began splitting the player base. Both Jack and George switched codes. Rugby league was already quite a different sport to rugby union. Interestingly, the groundwork for rugby league relations between the two countries was pioneered by a New Zealand Maori team the year before, just like the 1888 New Zealand Natives had done in the UK.

They are the only brothers to have played for both the All Blacks and Kiwis, a feat that is unlikely to be equalled any time soon.

The Spencers played in all three tests in the first series between the Kiwis and Australia, which was lost 2–1. They are the only brothers to have played for both the All Blacks and Kiwis, a feat that is unlikely to be equalled any time soon.

Of course, there may well have been some other brothers in that first decade of inter-code rivalry, but World War I started in 1914 and disrupted everyone's careers (not to mention millions of lives). Jimmy and Eddie Ryan might well have played together in the All Blacks instead of serving in the war, along with any number of the six other brothers in the Ryan family who also played for Wellington. Instead, Jimmy's international career lasted until 1914, while Eddie waited until 1921 to get his one and only game against New South Wales.

However, Jimmy Ryan does have the distinction of captaining a New Zealand representative side to the first-ever international trophy win in 1919. Having served in the army, he led a New Zealand Services team to win the post-war King's Cup—a kind of proto-World Cup that involved army teams from all the Commonwealth Nations.

The 1920s are a pretty confusing time for rugby. The Great War had disrupted everything so much that some test matches are counted in some countries and not others. Player numbers in the UK had taken a gigantic hit due to the slaughter of the British middle and upper classes on the battlefield. Matches were scheduled while other New Zealand representative sides were away touring, which meant that player turnover during this time was huge. If anyone these days complains about the supposed 'cheapening of the All Blacks jersey', the 1920s provides a good riposte if you want to demonstrate that the 'more the merrier' approach to selection is really nothing new.

Ces Badeley could claim he invented the cross-kick, which led to Jack Steel's stunning try in the 1921 first test against the Springboks.

Because of that, a few more sets of brothers were added to the list of All Blacks. Jack and Sydney (Syd) Shearer both played games against New South Wales in 1920–21. Fred and Jim Tilyard did the same, with Fred being another player to have his war service interrupt a career that spanned seven years but only 10 games for the All Blacks. Ces Badeley could claim he invented the cross-kick, which led to Jack Steel's stunning try in the 1921 first test against the Springboks. Ces's brother Victor played for the 1922 All Blacks, but the games he played against New South Wales don't count as tests.

Ces then went on to be selected for the 1924–25 Invincibles

tour, but was injured and played only a handful of games. Quentin Donald from Wairarapa, who would later get himself sent off for attempting to stare down Maurice Brownlie in a game against Hawke's Bay, was on the tour as well. His brother Jim then captained an entirely new All Blacks side that was picked when the triumphant team returned home.

It was on that tour that one of the most prominent All Blacks first fives ever added another chapter to his prolific career. Wellington's Mark Nicholls was one of the driving forces behind the team's success, and scored 284 points in his All Blacks career across 51 games and 10 tests. He had two brothers who, for reasons that have clearly gone out of fashion since the turn of the century, were named Harry and Harold. To make life easier for everyone, Harry was known as 'Ginger' and Harold, 'Doc'. Unlike their illustrious younger brother, both played only a handful of games for the All Blacks, and Ginger ended up going on the Invincibles tour as a hanger-on. Legend has it that Ginger started a romance with a girl in the UK by lying to her and saying he was star midfielder Bert Cooke. Things came to a head when the girl's father cornered the real Cooke with the intention of demanding that he marry her, which led to Cooke discovering what Ginger had been up to and knocking him out during what was supposed to be a friendly bout of blindfold boxing.

Laurie and Arthur Knight were another pair that probably should have played more tests, because their games against New South Wales should have been against Australia in 1925 and '26. Arthur finally did get a test call-up in 1934 when the Aussies put their national side back together. Bill Hadley was part of that team too, while his brother Swinbourne had gone on the first-ever tour to South Africa with the 1928 All Blacks.

The infamous moment when Cyril Brownlie became the first player to be sent off in the history of test rugby. His brother Maurice is among the All Blacks teammates watching on. **PHOTOSPORT**

MAURICE AND CYRIL BROWNLIE

NEW ZEALAND, LIKE MUCH OF the former British Empire, was awash with nostalgia over its role in the Great War as the hundredth anniversary of each battle took place over the years between 2014 and 2018. It was, on one hand, an introspective look at our contribution to the conflict as a small nation of just over a million people. On the other hand, it was four years of cherry-picking the most convenient history to fit our common narrative. Gallipoli and Passchendaele got all the attention, as that's where the highest amount of casualties occurred, and we rehashed some questionable themes about how our brave boys were sent off to die by incompetent British generals. Not to mention confusingly hypocritical messaging about the importance of sacrificing one's life for one's country, while at the same time saying the war was an avoidable tragedy.

We didn't hear much about what happened in Sinai and Palestine, though. That's not surprising, given that it barely got any press at the time either. Maybe we just like talking about heroic failures, because the campaign in the desert, spearheaded by the New Zealand Mounted Rifles Brigade, was one of the most successful New Zealand military operations of all time.

It involved a family whose name would become one of the most famous to ever wear the All Blacks jersey. And one of the most infamous.

On 15 February 1915, Anthony 'Tony' Brownlie walked into a recruitment office in Napier and signed up to fight in World War I. By now, New Zealand had been part of the action for five and a half months. Despite the shockingly high casualty rates from the Western Front—France had lost around 300,000 men already—the ANZACs were in Egypt and in high spirits. They were yet to go into battle, the landings on Gallipoli were still a couple of months away and time was being spent training for what was supposed to be a quick incursion inland on the peninsula. This was going to be the campaign that would make all the difference in a conflict that was now spreading a lot further than anyone had expected.

Tony was 24 years old. His brothers Cyril and Maurice would eventually follow him into uniform. The younger two are the ones you've probably heard of, and the bulk of this story will be about them—but in order to understand their motivations and journey it's essential to include how they were affected by the war and growing up in New Zealand in that time. First of all, this wasn't the Brownlie brothers' first brush with a death in the family.

Their mother, Nora, had died of blood poisoning in 1900, before Tony had turned 10. She and father James had had seven children before she passed: two daughters, Clare and Grace, and two other sons, Louie and Jack Laurence, who was dubbed 'Laurie'.

The family settled in Whanganui while the children grew up. In 1903, little Louie was killed aged only four, when a horse trap fell on him while he was playing on it.

James sent the four remaining boys to boarding school. In an odd turn of events, Tony was sent to St Patrick's College in Wellington, while the other three went north to attend Sacred Heart College in Auckland. However, after only a year, Maurice and Laurie joined Tony at St Pat's, while Cyril stayed on at Sacred Heart. All of them played cricket and rugby throughout their school years.

Tony left school in 1909 and by 1912 was playing senior club rugby. His form was good enough for him to be picked for the Whanganui side. By 1913, James had remarried and shifted the family across the North Island to Hawke's Bay. All the boys stayed with the family, as James needed the extra manpower to farm the land he'd purchased in Petane. The next year, though, saw war break out.

Tony wasted little time in joining up with the New Zealand Mounted Rifles Brigade, in a time when horses were still integral to military operations. The Sinai and Palestine campaign would cover an area of around 4000 square miles that stretched from the Suez Canal in the south to Aleppo in the north, but when he joined the war in June 1915 it was at the tail end of the Gallipoli campaign. The ANZACs had barely made a foothold on the landing beaches and the Mounted Rifles' horses were put to other uses while their riders simply filled up the trenches like everyone else. They had suffered terrible losses—all of the Auckland, Wellington and Canterbury regiments had been halved in number.

Within a couple of months, Gallipoli would be abandoned and the entire ANZAC force would head back across the clear waters of the Mediterranean to the sands of the Egyptian desert.

It was in these wide open expanses that the Mounted Rifles' proper military capability proved itself to be a far cry from the stalemate happening in Europe. They would ride into battle on horseback, but they weren't cavalry. Clad in woollen uniforms and iconic slouch hats, they would dismount and engage their Ottoman enemies with a .303 rifle or Vickers machine gun. Tony was assigned to a new unit of the Mounted Rifles in 1916, the Machine Gun Squadron, which was around 230 men strong. They worked in sections of half a dozen—two to operate the gun itself, the rest to provide covering fire and carry ammunition. Trooper N. W. H. Beaven, writing for the *Kia Ora Coo-ee* (a newspaper for soldiers stationed in the Middle East), remembered:

> Carrying a machine gun into action is no joke. The order has been given 'Dismount. Guns off!' You leap off, hand your horse over to your pack leader, bundle the gun and tripod off the pack and then find that the enemy is much farther away than you thought. If you are No 1 you shoulder the tripod, if No 2 the gun, whilst Nos. 3 and 4 take two boxes of ammunition each from one of the ammunition packs: and off you start to the nearest vantage spot to get the gun into business. The section officer or sergeant to the leader or perhaps the scout has been sent forward to select a spot, and you plod wearily on with bullets zipping all around.

It was fast, furious fighting in inhospitable terrain. Holding a position near a water source was a matter of life or death. Getting lost in the desert was just a matter of death.

Cyril joined up not long after his older brother in 1915, at age 20. He left New Zealand after three months of basic training and found himself in the desert with the Machine Gun Squadron of the Mounted Rifles as well. Instead of the battles and medals of which he was probably dreaming when he signed up back home, and in what was a foreshadowing of the incident he is most associated with, he frequently found himself in trouble with his superiors. Cyril was found guilty of insolence towards an NCO and punished with hard labour in 1917. He didn't miss much in the way of combat. The Mounted Rifles spent the better part of 1917 locked in a stalemate in the Negev Desert, where they mostly battled the harsh living conditions.

Maurice was the last to enlist, after he turned 20 in 1916. He too joined his brothers in the same unit, and made his way to Egypt in April 1917. By now the Mounted Rifles' battle honours included securing the Suez Canal, the Battle of Romani and the destruction of the Ottoman garrison at Rafa.

The battle to capture the village of Ayun Kara took place on 14 November 1917. It was the latest contact with the Ottomans as the Mounted Rifles Brigade, along with three Australian Light Horse Brigades that made up the Australian and New Zealand Mounted Division of the Egyptian Expeditionary Force (EEF), broke out and pursued the Ottomans up northward through what today makes up modern-day Israel. The EEF was around 300,000 men strong. They'd hit their enemy at Gaza and Beersheeba a fortnight before, driving towards Jerusalem.

Gaza had been a bloody offensive, with Australian trooper Ion Idriess writing in his diary: 'Our infantry failed in their attacks, but only the English generals are to blame. No doubt they have their reasons for their different movements, but those reasons lost the day, for the time being at least. And now many more men must die before we take Gaza.'

By the time they had overrun the city, total EEF casualties for the campaign had reached 28,000. The outward objective was to push the Ottoman Empire back across the desert and vanquish an ally of the Central Powers. Behind the scenes, though, it was also an excellent opportunity for the British to expand their considerable influence over a region rich in the now vital commodity of oil.

While the EEF fought their way up through the Levant, they had the Arab Revolt raging on their right flank throughout the Middle East, making the conflict they were engaged in probably the most far-reaching of the whole war.

One veteran—trooper Ben Gainsford, quoted in Glyn Harper's 2016 book *Johnny Enzed*—described Ayun Kara as 'our best scrap. We lost a lot of good men.' The official NZMR report called it 'the most severe engagement of the campaign'. The entire Mounted Rifles Brigade was involved that day. Among those who saddled up and made the advance was 18-year-old Johnstone 'Jock' Richardson, a promising rugby player from Otago who had lied about his age when he'd enlisted the year before.

The Mounted Rifles Brigade attacked the village from the south with a force of around 800 men, trying to encircle the Ottoman defenders, who held fortified positions on a ridge about a mile in length. The Wellington and Auckland regiments pressed forward to take the high ground, while the Canterbury men became engaged to the east in a tangle of orange groves. What was supposed to be a quick fight against a rearguard force quickly turned into a major engagement. The entire brigade was mobilised to take out an Ottoman force numbering around 1500.

The battle hinged on one moment. A decision was made to take out a key machine-gun position on the right side of the ridge. The Wellington Regiment stormed forward over two kilometres of open ground, then dismounted and fixed bayonets. They overran the position, then turned the guns on the Ottomans, opening up the opportunity for the Auckland Regiment to close in and rout the remaining defenders, who fled northward.

The engagement had lasted around two and a half hours. The Mounted Rifles Brigade suffered 185 casualties, including 44 killed. The Ottoman losses were around 500 casualties, with 170 dead and 34 captured.

One of the troopers who fell was Sergeant Tony Brownlie. In a sad twist of fate, his death came when he was away from the main fighting, caught by a stray bullet while he was having his ammunition refilled. Richardson was there when he died, and watched the stretcher-bearers take his body away. 'It was terrible and so unexpected, even in the midst of all that war,' he later said. Cyril and Maurice learned the news while training in Egypt.

By the end of the year, the EEF had taken Jerusalem. Cyril and Maurice spent the rest of the war riding the desert, involved in the sort of brief skirmishes that characterised the campaign. They played together in the Mounted Rifles rugby team, and Maurice won an army boxing title. There's no evidence that either was involved in the Surafend Massacre in December 1918, after the war had ended, in which Australian and New Zealand mounted troops destroyed a village and slaughtered all the male inhabitants as a reprisal for one of their men being killed in a failed robbery attempt by a local.

As in any theatre of conflict, the deadliest enemy wasn't the bullets and shells of the enemy soldiers, but disease.

Cyril had been seriously ill with malaria in Palestine, and had even been told he'd never be able to play rugby again. Maurice had also had to spend time in hospital recuperating from illness, and hadn't been as much a thorn in the side of his superiors as Cyril. In fact, before he would return home he was promoted to corporal. The Brownlie brothers also had to contend with the threat of the influenza epidemic sweeping the world at the end of the conflict.

The illnesses were probably one of the reasons why, when Cyril and Maurice were demobilised and returned to New Zealand in

1919, neither went back out on a rugby field for a couple of years.

Tony's death was the latest tragedy that the Brownlie brothers had to deal with, but the family had grown larger in their absence. James and stepmother Ethel had three more sons while the brothers were away at war: Ralph, and twins Jack and Jim.

Younger brother Laurie, meanwhile, had been too young to serve in the war. By 1921, he was definitely old enough to play senior rugby, and did well enough to be selected for Hawke's Bay. Then get named in the North Island team. Then an All Blacks trial. It's somewhat unbelievable now to think that a player had such a quick ascent to that level, but the way teams were picked back then was very different to the way they do now—which both Cyril and Maurice would find out later on as well.

The way the All Blacks games were scheduled was quite far removed from these days, too. The first-ever Springbok team to visit New Zealand arrived in 1921, but while the tour was going on, an entirely different All Blacks side played New South Wales in Christchurch in between the third and fourth tests. Australian rugby was still pulling itself together after the war, with Queensland more or less abandoning the code for the time being. So instead of a national side, the NSW rep team was sent. Laurie was picked as a back-row forward (positions were still dictated by the prevailing 2–3–2 scrum formation), which the All Blacks promptly lost 17–0. That's actually a lot worse than the scoreline suggests from a modern point of view, and remains one of the worst defeats in All Blacks history. It speaks volumes that the anomaly of a game was granted test status by Australia's rugby union but not New Zealand's.

It was Laurie's first game in a black jersey. It was also his last. The next year, he blew out his knee, causing him to make only sporadic appearances at club level for the next few seasons. He finally retired in 1926.

While Laurie and the other one-game All Blacks who had their rear ends handed to them that day are part of an unwanted place in New Zealand rugby history, James Brownlie was proud of his son. So proud, he issued his famous ultimatum to Cyril and Maurice: 'If Laurie can win New Zealand honours, so can you two.'

The good news for James, and the All Blacks, is that the older brothers took his threat seriously and began forging careers that would take them exactly where their father envisaged. Cyril and Maurice played for the Hastings club and both enjoyed similarly swift paths up the chain to representative rugby. Both, like Laurie, were big loose forwards standing over six feet tall and weighing around 100 kilograms. Cyril had a fair complexion, blonde, with slightly angular features. Maurice was square-jawed, dark-haired and handsome.

By 1922, both were in the Hawke's Bay team that beat Wellington for the Ranfurly Shield. Later in the season, Maurice was picked for the North Island team (the inter-island rugby fixtures were an important part of talent identification and would remain that way for many years), then the All Blacks trial. At the end of July that year, he found himself on a boat heading across the Tasman with the All Blacks.

Once again, the All Blacks were taking on New South Wales. Maurice would have been keen to make up for the time Laurie played against them the year before, and they won the first test 26–19. However, the next two were defeats and the series was lost. Like Laurie's debut, these games are confusingly regarded as tests by the Australians and not the All Blacks, and it would take another two years and a trip halfway around the world for

Maurice to make his official test debut. By then, his brother would join him. By now, both had established reputations on the field— although Cyril's was, like his wartime discipline record, a telling reminder that he was prone to getting himself on the wrong side of the referees.

'[Maurice] is the sort of forward that has usurped the common garden variety forward that held sway in his place a few years back. Brownlie is a magnificent type of player that has all the weight necessary, yet is as fast as a deer,' said a remarkably quaint review in the *New Zealand Truth*. Later in the same piece, this was said of Cyril: 'Cyril has one bad habit, and he will have to drop it pronto. He is inclined to go for a man when he has got rid of the ball. This can be easily mistaken for dirty play and at Home he will find himself in hot water if he should come at it.'

'Home' meant the United Kingdom. The All Blacks were scheduled to tour there in 1924–25, and both Brownlie brothers were in the squad after strong showings for Hawke's Bay and the North Island teams. Both brothers were picked in the All Blacks to play three games as a warm-up for the tour against, you guessed it, New South Wales, where Cyril's first experience in a black jersey was a loss. They ended up winning the next two and returned to New Zealand to prepare for the 32-match tour of the UK.

The squad contained 11 war veterans. Four were members of the Mounted Rifles: Jim Parker had been in the same Machine Gun Squadron as the Brownlie brothers, as had now 25-year-old Jock Richardson.

Another veteran was Southlander Andrew 'Son' White, who had the distinction (or misfortune, depending how you want to look at it) of being involved in almost the entire war, having signed up at the outbreak in 1914. He'd landed on Gallipoli with the NZEF, then went on to the Western Front until June 1918. The sort of horror he witnessed in the trenches had driven him to drink and to go absent without leave, then violently defend himself against one of the military policemen sent to apprehend him. Like Cyril, he was disciplined—but much more harshly. White was sentenced to a brutal practice known as Field Punishment Number One—tied to a post every day for four weeks. As was typical of military discipline of the time, it had the complete opposite effect of what was intended. When he was finally released, White was so psychologically ruined that he was ruled as being no longer fit for service and was sent back to New Zealand. It's somewhat of a miracle given the lack of rehabilitation assistance at the time that he'd managed to rebuild himself both physically and mentally to become an All Black.

Tellingly, 10 of the 11 men who'd gone to war were forwards. By now, Cyril was 29 and Maurice 28, and there was a decent age gap between Maurice and the youngest member of the team. However, 19-year-old fullback George Nepia would have been well known to the brothers by now. He'd broken into the Hawke's Bay team in 1922 and clearly held the brothers in a fair degree of awe.

It's somewhat of a miracle given the lack of rehabilitation assistance at the time that he'd managed to rebuild himself both physically and mentally to become an All Black.

In Nepia's autobiography, he described Maurice as being 'the handsomest of men and I think perhaps the strongest man I have ever seen'. As for Cyril: 'He is rather less formidable as a personality than Maurice, perhaps because he does not take life quite as seriously.'

Nepia was to go on to cement his name as one of the greatest All Blacks ever on the tour. He had an armchair view from his position at the back of the Brownlies and the rest of the forwards rampaging their way through the opposition in the team that was to become known as 'The Invincibles'. However, that's certainly not the perception the New Zealand press had of them before they boarded ship and left. It also hadn't helped that after the New South Wales series, the All Blacks had lost a game to Auckland on their return.

This was a unique period for All Blacks rugby. The war had brought the international game to a shuddering halt. Rugby was very much in rebuilding mode worldwide, and there was little hard evidence as to how strong the national sides actually were. After all, the nearest international opponent couldn't even scrape a team together to call the Wallabies, but was able to beat the All Blacks on a fairly regular basis. Travel by boat across the Tasman alone would take several days, and it's not as though anyone could simply watch footage of each other playing.

Low expectations or not, it was the first All Blacks side to visit Britain since 1905, and they had revenge on their minds. The loss to Wales in 1905, which was the All Blacks' only blemish of that entire tour, was thought of as the underarm incident of its day, thanks to a referee unable to keep up with the play in his dress shoes. This was the test that the 1924 side wanted desperately to win, to balance the ledger.

The journey on the steamer *Remuera* took months. The ship made a stop at Pitcairn Island, then headed north-east through the Panama Canal and across the Atlantic. Nepia said that the team organised an orchestra, in which Maurice played the kazoo. They trained on the deck and lost a couple of balls overboard that are probably still floating somewhere in the Pacific Ocean.

The woefully undersized home side look like a bunch of dead men walking, some not even bothering to take their hands out of their pockets.

Any talk of the All Blacks being not up to scratch was dispelled in the first few weeks of the tour. It took until the fifth game before they even conceded their first points, and even then their opponents Swansea found themselves on the other end of a 39–3 scoreline. They looked to be on track to emulate their 1905 counterparts at the very least. Maurice and Cyril had already started the way they intended to continue, throwing their big frames around the field and impressing onlookers with their willingness to run the ball. By the time they played Durham the effect their reputation was having on their opposition was obvious. Newsreel footage of the two sides taking the field shows the All Blacks confidently marching onto the park with their sleeves rolled up as if off to another day at work. The woefully undersized home side look like a bunch of dead men walking, some not even bothering to take their hands out of their pockets. For the record, the All Blacks flogged Durham 43–5 that day.

The team arrived in Dublin for their first test match. Nepia notes in his book that it was an eerie place to be in 1924—the Irish Civil War had ended only the previous year and the O'Connell Street post office, a giant classical-style stone edifice, was still a bombed-out shell after years of fighting. Many more buildings were riddled with bullet and artillery holes, so the reaction of the All Blacks who had been too young to go to war would have been a marked contrast to those who had. The test against the Irish was a low-scoring affair, with the All Blacks winning 6–0. Maurice was the only Brownlie who played.

The next test was the much-anticipated match against the Welsh back in Swansea. Maurice took it upon himself to tear the game the All Blacks' way by scoring a rampaging solo try in the twenty-fifth minute to give them an 8–0 lead. Cyril, on his test debut, nearly scored as well. The All Blacks, by now, were an efficiently oiled machine and were not going to allow any repeat of the 1905 robbery. Final score 19–0; the only international side that the All Blacks hadn't beaten had been thrashed convincingly. Now, on to London for a date with England.

Spirits were high. The Wales test was the big game of the tour, but England were the current Five Nations champions and hadn't lost a game in two seasons. This was a chance to make a statement at the home of the game itself in front of the biggest crowd of the entire tour. The upstart colonials, written off by their own press just months previously, were in the sort of form that could demolish the best of the British Isles just as the calendar ticked over into 1925.

That's what the test should have been remembered for, because that's what the All Blacks did. From start to finish they pummelled the English. The final score was 17–11, but it should have been a lot more. No one who was there was in any doubt about who was the superior side. Especially because the All Blacks did it with only 14 men for 73 minutes of the game.

That's the reason the 1925 test against England is so well

remembered. It's a story that's been told so many times it's become a confusing collection of memories, conjecture and moralising. One thing is for certain, though. Cyril Brownlie became the first test rugby player ever to get sent off. Exactly what he did is up for some serious interpretation. The incident in question was in a ruck near the touchline.

After sifting through the evidence, it seems that at best Cyril was the victim of either a referee determined to stamp his authority on the game, or a case of mistaken identity. At worst, he'd punched or even kicked a guy in the mouth and then lipped off at the ref when he was pinged for it. The man in charge that day was Albert Freethy of Wales, who had controlled the All Blacks' win over Ireland. He claimed later that he'd cautioned Cyril against rough play—something that doesn't really stack up given that only seven minutes of play had passed. Whatever happened, the English player who got up with his face the worse for wear was supposedly flanker Tom Voyce. He apparently told Freethy of the alleged strike, but even that is disputable.

A report in the *New Zealand Truth* stated:

> Mr Freethy could not name the England player reported by him as being kicked. There is no evidence of any player actually being on the ground at that time . . . And from information received from most reliable quarters it appears Cyril Brownlie was not one of those players previously cautioned. Actually it was Maurice Brownlie who had been spoken to.

Maybe the sort of attitude Cyril had harboured back in the deserts of Egypt that had him clapped in irons and forced to do hard labour finally erupted again. One of the English players testified that Cyril told Freethy just what he thought of his decision to penalise him and that sealed his fate, which isn't backed up by the referee himself. Or maybe he was just incredibly unlucky. All Blacks manager Stan Dean said, 'I had a long chat afterwards with Mr Freethy and asked him point-blank who it was who Cyril Brownlie had deliberately kicked. The referee said he did not know.'

The All Blacks captain that day was none other than Jock Richardson. He'd already watched one Brownlie brother die, and was now witnessing the potential lifetime disgracing of another. Richardson pleaded with Freethy, and English captain Wavell Wakefield, to let Cyril stay on the field. Wakefield, himself a veteran officer of the Royal Naval Air Service, claimed he couldn't hear Richardson's pleas because he was wearing headgear. Out of all the components in the story, that's probably the least likely.

So far, so confusing. Laws these days are hard enough to get your head around, but having a player sent off for something that no one could agree on is ridiculous. Still, it had an undoubtedly galvanising effect on the rest of the All Blacks. Nepia's account of how it went down, in a chapter of his autobiography tellingly entitled 'Never Forgotten, Never Forgiven', is emotional to say the least:

> I can see myself running up to protest, Wakefield grimly shaking his head and turning away when Richardson approaches him to intercede, the rest of us bewilderedly asking for an explanation. And still Brownlie is trudging from us. There are 60,000 people in the ground and not one of them can even whisper. The silence is so weird as to be

almost frightening. Brownlie goes from us. We come upon him later, at half-time, in the dressing room. He is sitting on a bench, still in his togs. Brownlie has been a soldier and a farmer, as both he has become inured to the circle of life and death that governs our lives. He is a big, mature, powerful man. Yet the tears are rolling down his cheeks. You carry that lump in your throat for the rest of your life when you think of him sitting there in his loneliness.

All Blacks first five Mark Nicholls was scathing of Freethy:

> I am not going to be so unwise to say that everything was fair and above board, because I know it wasn't, but to single out one man from sixteen guilty ones was, to my mind, unfair and showed discrimination. Mr Freethy was a wonderful referee, but in what should have been his greatest triumph, the greatest match of his career, he made a scapegoat of a great footballer and gentleman, when he himself was at fault.

The team responded by turning in its most memorable performance of the tour. Wakefield, hard of hearing or not, and his team found out first-hand how ruthless the All Blacks can be when they get angry and found themselves down 9–3 at half-time. But it didn't go exactly according to plan; winger Jack Steel was injured after scoring the All Blacks' second try and played little part in the rest of the game. It really made no difference, in the end. Midfielder Bert Cooke summed up the attitude of the All Blacks: 'We were to avenge the unjust charge made against Brownlie . . . and a new spirit seemed to obsess us.'

The All Blacks ferociously tore into every ruck and maul. While the English defence did hold up enough to stop the game becoming a complete rout, and brought some credibility to their claim of being the best side in Europe, the result was never in doubt.

Bert Cooke summed up the attitude of the All Blacks: 'We were to avenge the unjust charge made against Brownlie . . . and a new spirit seemed to obsess us.'

But the most epic moment of justice came in the second half. Maurice got his hands on the ball at the spot where his brother had walked off Twickenham in disgrace. There was about 25 metres and three defenders between him and the English goal line, but it wouldn't have mattered if there'd been a brick wall and armed guards. In a scene that would be emulated by Colin Meads and Jonah Lomu, Maurice ploughed his way to the line and slammed the ball down to make the game safe. While the home side pulled back a couple of points, the win over England with a man down for almost the entire match remains one of the greatest All Blacks performances of all time.

The Brownlie brothers were at the forefront. Cyril's send-off and Maurice's subsequent revenge-inspired display are what both men are most well remembered for in All Blacks lore—rightly or wrongly. The win was another milestone symbolic of New Zealand's rugby relationship with Britain that persists to this day: massively one-sided results, while constantly being accused of somehow cheating and being the 'bad guys'.

However, it didn't overshadow the fact that the All Blacks had consistently smashed everyone put up against them, tacking on a few hidings in France and Canada after they left the UK and writing another chapter in the team's young but already formidable reputation. By the time they returned home, they'd been dubbed The Invincibles. Maurice had scored 11 tries on the 32-match tour, Cyril 10.

They were met with a heroes' welcome, and both slotted straight back into their all-conquering Hawke's Bay team which had held the Ranfurly Shield since 1922. The team then went about forging what was the first-ever proper dynasty in the iconic trophy's history. The next All Blacks tour wasn't until 1928, so the seasons in between saw Maurice and Cyril mainly concentrate on helping their provincial union maintain the dominance it exerted over the rest of the country.

Hawke's Bay spent 1926 racking up the sort of scores that wouldn't look out of place in a one-sided Super Rugby game. Their southern neighbours Wairarapa were smashed 77–14, then traditional powerhouses Wellington and Auckland were sent packing to the tune of 58–8 and 41–11.

However, everything came to a shuddering halt a year later when they lost a couple of their All Blacks. George Nepia had headed up to East Coast. Bert Cooke, who by now had carved out a reputation that would see him regarded as one of the best centres to ever play for the All Blacks, switched unions from Hawke's Bay to Wairarapa. His new side, which had been so comprehensively embarrassed the year before, eventually rectified their 1926 thrashing and won the Ranfurly Shield off Hawke's Bay in June of that year. The game ended 15–11 to the challengers, but it should be noted that a great deal of Bay supporters felt it was time that the Shield changed hands anyway.

Fast forward a few months, and they'd definitely changed their minds. The rematch saw thousands of supporters travel south to Masterton, to watch a game that would go down as one of the most controversial in New Zealand rugby history. While what was known as the 'Battle of Solway' is mostly remembered for the sensational aftermath, it did provide a unique role reversal for the Brownlie brothers.

Two years after Cyril had been sent off in that test win, it was Maurice's turn to have an early shower in an equally epic Ranfurly Shield game. With eerily similar timing to Cyril's send-off, the younger brother had an altercation with his Invincibles teammate Quentin Donald, the Wairarapa front-row forward. According to the *New Zealand Times*:

> Donald came through a ruck and ran into the arms of Brownlie. No blows were struck, but the pair glared at each other. The referee, no doubt deeming the game would get out of hand if he did not firmly maintain control, made a motion of dismissal to both players and the two All Blacks who had stood shoulder to shoulder on many hard-fought fields in Britain and France in 1924 had to make their way to the sideline.

So, unlike Cyril's moment of infamy, it was clear-cut what had happened. But it's a drastic move to order two players from the field for simply glaring at one another. Perhaps the referee was worried about the potential ramifications for Donald if a scrap had occurred—the Wairarapa player was giving away a lot in terms of height and weight advantage to Maurice, the former army boxing champion. However, just like at Twickenham, the other Brownlie brother was on hand to make amends.

Now it was Cyril's turn to dish out the revenge. He tore around the Solway Park field with the sort of manic devotion to victory that Maurice had against the English. Merely winning the Shield back wasn't enough for Cyril; he ending up having one of the best games of his career in what eventually was a 21–10 win for Hawke's Bay.

Apparently, given that the double send-off wasn't caused by any real act of violence and there weren't any other fights of note, the game itself shouldn't really have been called a 'Battle'. It was probably cooked up before the match had even kicked off, given that the magnitude of the occasion made it arguably the most anticipated provincial match thus far. The 'Battle of Solway' better describes what happened after in the chambers of the NZRFU. Hawke's Bay were alleged to have fielded an ineligible player (anyone involved at club rugby long enough would know all about this sort of thing), and after a good deal of provincial squabbling, they were stripped of the Shield. In one small consolation and historical anomaly, it didn't head back to Wairarapa, but to the combined union of Manawhenua. They'd beaten Wairarapa in a 'challenge' while the whole mess got sorted out.

Later in 1927, both brothers were selected to trial for the All Blacks tour to South Africa the following year. (This is another real sign of the times; teams were regularly picked up to a year in advance.) They were, still, instantly recognisable figures at a time when New Zealand had few celebrities. The larger-than-life brothers that represented the nation would both travel to South Africa in 1928, the first tour the All Blacks would make there.

Sadly, they would be without George Nepia. Despite apartheid officially not being instituted for another two decades, Māori were told they weren't welcome. In a scenario that would play out again in the future, the NZRFU simply accepted the edict and sent a team without some of their best players. Jimmy Mill and Wattie Barclay would both be denied the right to play against the Springboks as well. Bert Cooke couldn't get time off work for the tour. The players' absence would be keenly felt.

Maurice was made captain for what would become the last series of his career—a scenario that would be repeated when the final curtain came for Colin Meads, the player he would most be compared to. For maybe the first time in his life Maurice was able to sit in the front row of the team photo, cutting a massively asymmetrical figure alongside the assorted backs to the left and right of his sinewy arms. Hopes were high that the team would sweep through South Africa like the Invincibles had through the UK, but the All Blacks were about to find out that this was going to be one nut they wouldn't be able to crack. In fact, not for the next 68 years.

The first test in Durban was one for the record books, and not in a good way. The 17–0 defeat remains to this day the All Blacks' heaviest-ever loss to the Springboks, and was their highest margin of defeat in all test matches until 1999. Hardly the dream start to Maurice's captaincy. The news was greeted in New Zealand like some sort of natural disaster, and he wasn't helped by the team's manager, Boer War veteran Bill Hornig, who kept dropping dreadfully unsuitable anecdotes at after-match functions about the last time he'd been in South Africa.

Maurice played in 18 games on the tour, including four tests. For Cyril, though, the entire trip was a frustrating exercise. He fell ill and could only take the field in half a dozen games. His physical presence was missed as the All Blacks and Springboks belted each other around the park.

Fortunately, the test series wasn't a complete write-off. Two out of the remaining three tests were won. The contest between the two leading teams in the world now hung in the balance for the time being—it would not have a decisive blow landed until the Springboks returned to New Zealand in 1937.

Maurice's career ended with a win—a series-saving 13–5 result in Cape Town. Cyril's last game in black was against Orange Free State.

By now Cyril was 33 and Maurice 32. Both were ready to hang up their boots and return to their farms and work the land, something they would likely have been doing all along had it not been for their father's challenge to them to emulate their younger brother. Maurice had already had a highly publicised and ultimately ill-fated romance and engagement with English silent movie star Marie Ney, and from that he learned that it was probably best to marry a local girl if he wanted to have a content life in his rural environment. He and Maude Barker were hitched in 1930, and they had two daughters. Legend has it that Maurice would wear his All Blacks blazer to dinner every Sunday evening. Cyril married Molly Jefferson, and had three children.

The on-field story of the Brownlie brothers doesn't finish here—well not quite, anyway. There's still the matter of the three other brothers born while Cyril and Maurice were away at war. Jack, Jim and Ralph were all talented enough to play top-level club rugby by the time World War II broke out—then the conflict robbed them of their best playing years. Jim did go on to play a decent number of matches for Hawke's Bay up until 1948, while Jack was in and out of the team until 1949. Tragically, after Ralph had represented Hawke's Bay B just as the war started, he was killed aged 26 in 1943 while training in the RNZAF.

Cyril and Maurice both passed away relatively young. Cyril was working on his farm when he collapsed and died in 1954 aged 59, and Maurice followed in 1957 aged 60.

You're not going to find many rugby stories that begin in the deserts of Egypt, then go through Twickenham and one of the most controversial incidents in the history of the game.

But this is it. Cyril, Maurice, Laurie and Tony Brownlie's tale goes across the world and back again, bound by brotherhood and the game of rugby. They lived in a time so far removed from the one we live in now, it's hard to get a gauge on what sort of people they were, how they lived their lives, and what influenced their decisions. One thing is for sure: the acts of the lesser-known Brownlie brothers profoundly affected Cyril and Maurice. Had it not been for Tony, they may never have ended up in the Palestinian desert. Had it not been for Laurie, they may never have ended up in the All Blacks.

> **You're not going to find many rugby stories that begin in the deserts of Egypt, then go through Twickenham and one of the most controversial incidents in the history of the game.**

Tony is buried at Ramleh War Cemetery, south-east of Tel Aviv, alongside other New Zealanders who lost their lives in the two world wars. Ayun Kara, like the cemetery where he lies, is now part of Israel. The battle, which was a resounding victory for the Mounted Rifles Brigade, remains relatively unknown in

New Zealand. There are a couple of clips on YouTube about it that have a few hundred views each.

Maurice is regarded as one of the greatest All Blacks to ever pick up a rugby ball. He was a giant of a man in both stature and reputation, his 61 games for the team a record for 28 years after his retirement.

There is no footage captured of whatever Cyril did to get sent off against England, although there is one iconic photograph of him leaving the field. He deserves to be remembered for more than that. Like his brother, he was a tough, strong, no-nonsense player that took part in some of the most glorious days of All Blacks and Hawke's Bay rugby.

The place where he was ordered off, Twickenham, is arguably the centre of the rugby world. It hosted the 2015 World Cup final, 90 years after Albert Freethy made his fateful ruling. The All Blacks that day played like their 1925 counterparts, leaving the field champions of the world. They'd never dare call themselves Invincible, though. That honour belongs solely to the men of the Brownlie generation.

Frank (left) and Dave Solomon
were trailblazers for Pacific
Island rugby in New Zealand.
NEW ZEALAND RUGBY MUSEUM

FRANK AND
DAVE SOLOMON

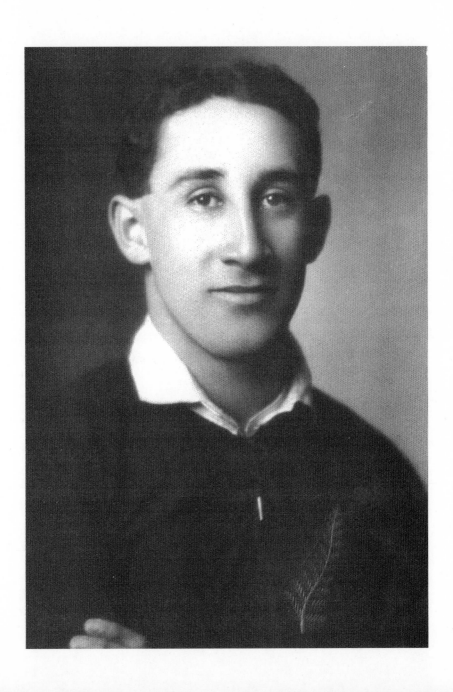

IF THERE'S ONE THING THAT gets under the skin of New Zealand rugby fans and administrators, it's the word 'poaching'. Taking talent from the Pacific Islands to bolster our own teams, as if men sent by New Zealand Rugby sneak into villages in Samoa, Tonga and Fiji in the middle of the night and chloroform locals, only for them to wake up wearing an Auckland jersey in the middle of Eden Park in front of the All Blacks selectors.

At least, that's what more or less any hack journalist or pub bore from the UK will tell you—and it isn't true. But while the reality of the situation these days isn't quite as innocent as New Zealand and its schooling system would like to portray, it's obvious that the folks in the northern hemisphere making those claims possess very little knowledge of New Zealand's role as a prime emigration point for Pacific Islanders.

Frank Solomon was born in the newly formed territory of American Samoa in 1906. His father took him to Fiji and remarried, and their blended family contained his new stepbrother Dave, born in 1913. Soon after, they all moved to Auckland where the boys grew up and played for the iconic Ponsonby club.

Frank's debut for the All Blacks was an auspicious one. The team welcomed the newly re-formed Wallabies, which had spent 13 years fractured into state sides in the post-war period. Charles Bathurst, better known as Lord Bledisloe, the Governor-General of New Zealand, donated a special trophy to be played for between the two nations. He also named it after himself, which is fine considering it turned out to be one of the biggest cups in world sport and probably would have been quite expensive.

It was also the first and last time Frank would play a test match in the position of wing forward. Back then, forward packs were organised into whatever configuration any nation wanted, so New Zealand had played a seven-man, 2–3–2 formation scrum with the extra 'wing forward' detached to harass the inside backs and gain a somewhat unfair advantage. By the early '30s, though, moves were made to align all countries to the modern 3–4–1 scrum, which rendered the wing forward obsolete.

> **Bathurst, better known as Lord Bledisloe, donated a special trophy to be played for between the two nations. He also named it after himself, which is fine considering it turned out to be one of the biggest cups in world sport.**

Frank therefore became the first-known Samoan-born player to play for the All Blacks. (Walter Batty, born in Tonga, was the first Pacific Island-born All Black, debuting in 1928.) They won the first-ever Bledisloe Cup test 20–13 at Eden Park, and he was picked for the return tour in 1932. As was common up until World War II, the side played a warm-up match against Wellington before they left but unfortunately got comprehensively thrashed 36–23. Wellington winger Nelson Ball remains the only man to ever score four tries in a game against the All Blacks, which would have been sweet for him as he'd been dropped from the side that beat Australia the year before.

The All Blacks were punished in the press, too. In what is a retrospectively highly offensive opinion, it was claimed Frank was only there to lead the haka—despite the fact that he wasn't Māori (Frank had actually been selected for the New Zealand Maori team a few years earlier because no one bothered to check if he was Māori or not). He did end up not making the first test side, which was probably a good thing as the Wallabies turned the tables and won 22–17.

Nevertheless, the All Blacks managed to pick up their form and sweep through the rest of the tour unbeaten. Frank was recalled to play at his new position of number 8, and scored a try as the All Blacks squared the series with a 21–3 win in Brisbane. His tour ended with a then-record hiding of Western Districts; he again scored a try in the 63–15 win.

The 13–0 loss would be the largest margin of victory for the English for the next 76 years.

Not only was the tour done and dusted, but so was Frank's international career. He wasn't picked again, but that was mainly due to the fact that the All Blacks didn't have an international programme in 1933. A couple of years later the Solomon name would again feature on an All Blacks team sheet, though. Dave was picked for the 1935–36 tour of the UK as a first five.

As far as All Blacks tours go, this one wasn't particularly successful. As well as dropping a test to Wales, they also lost to England for the first time ever. The 13–0 loss would be the largest margin of victory for the English for the next 76 years. As well as those two, the All Blacks lost to Welsh club side Swansea, in which Dave played one of his eight tour games. After the tour, Dave's All Blacks career was done, too.

Nevertheless, both men returned to their club in Auckland to continue their incredibly valuable careers. Ponsonby was one of the leading clubs in the country and eventually became a hotbed of Pacific Island talent as immigration to Auckland increased rapidly in the post-war period. Frank played on until his forties, while Dave switched to league and was eventually selected for the 1939–40 Kiwis team. It meant he could return to the UK and make up for the failures of his All Blacks trip.

Unfortunately, Germany didn't factor in rugby league when it decided to invade Poland the day after the Kiwis beat St Helens in their first match. War was declared and the tour was cancelled, and the team were presumably on the lookout for U-boats as they hurriedly returned home by ship—so a number of them could enlist and head back in the other direction for a different kind of tour.

After the war, both brothers resumed their roles as leading figures in the growing Auckland Pacific Island community. Frank and Dave were appointed matai (chief), a distinction reserved for only the most respected members. They both lived long lives in Auckland, passing away in the 1990s.

They probably didn't know it at the time, but Frank and Dave Solomon were trailblazers for the Pacific influence in the All Blacks. The next Samoan star to wear the black jersey was Bryan Williams, who came through the same Ponsonby club to dominate the All Blacks wing for the 1970s. From that time on, generations of children born of Samoan, Tongan and

Fijian parents in their new home have become part of New Zealand culture and society—with rugby being one of the main benefactors.

But the Solomon brothers were there from the very start.

‘Super Sid’ Going in action against
the Springboks in 1976, a couple of
years after he’d played alongside
brother Ken. **PHOTOSPORT**

THE POST-WAR ERA

HERE'S A FUN FACT: WHO'S HELD the Ranfurly Shield for the longest period of time? No, it isn't the all-conquering Auckland side of the '80s and early '90s. In 1938, Southland won the Log o' Wood from Otago, and didn't give it back until 1947. Of course, in six of those nine years they didn't have to defend it—which was just one of the disruptions that World War II caused to the sport. It robbed a countless number of players of the best years of their careers, axed a planned test series and smeared the game in France with the stain of being the sport of the collaborationist Vichy regime.

For the All Blacks, though, it meant that things had to bumble along the way they did after the first war—waiting for the world to get put back together before test-match rugby slowly became a priority. Their only matches in 1946 and '47 were against Australia, and they didn't play at all in 1948.

Maybe that was one of the reasons why Otago's Jimmy Haig switched to league after the '46 series. The 21-year-old All Blacks halfback was lured to the Kiwi side that toured the UK in '47, but his older brother Laurie stayed with rugby union. Laurie was picked for the All Blacks for the three tests against the British Lions in 1950, then again made the tour to the UK in 1953. By then, Jimmy had become captain of the Kiwis and was part of the record 49–25 win over Australia in 1952.

Laurie missed selection for the 1949 series against the Springboks through injury. North Auckland war veteran Johnny Smith missed out because he was Māori. He'd played for the famous New Zealand Expeditionary Force team in 1945 and '46, also called the 'Kiwis', and was part of a tour through Britain to raise morale among the shattered and war-weary population. Later in '46, he was selected for the All Blacks alongside Jimmy Haig, and then in '47 he was joined in the All Blacks by his brother Peter. The Smiths became the first pair of post-war brothers to appear on the same field together, for the All Blacks in a tour match against Queensland, but Peter's All Blacks career ended after that tour.

Johnny, who played only four tests and nine games in total, has gone down as one of the greatest 'if onlys' of All Blacks history. He's widely regarded as the best midfield back of his time, and his name will always be included in the discussion of great All Blacks. It's also a name that gets brought up when the issue of sporting contact with South Africa is mentioned—Smith wasn't considered for selection on the first post-war tour due to apartheid and his absence is generally regarded as one of the reasons why the All Blacks were beaten 4–0 in the test series. Instead, Johnny stayed behind and played in an undermanned 'other' All Blacks team that was beaten twice by Australia.

In a supreme act of irony, Johnny Smith was awarded the inaugural Tom French Cup for being the outstanding Māori player of the year in 1949. He never played for the All Blacks again.

Maurice and Jack Goddard were two other war vets who came home to represent their country. Maurice finished his service in the air force to play in the Combined Services team, then for the All Blacks in '46. He too played on the '49 tour, and by then

Jack had made the touring side as well. While their All Blacks experience wasn't the most successful, both brothers played a leading hand in South Canterbury winning the Ranfurly Shield in 1950.

Bill Meates was another man who had served in North Africa and Italy before being drafted into the NZEF Kiwis, then spent his post-war years waiting for a call-up to the All Blacks. It came on the '49 tour, although his reputation survived the drubbing to be picked again the following season for all four tests against the British Lions. His younger brother Kevin played two tests against the Wallabies in 1952, then spent his later life trying to gain favour with Prime Minister Norman Kirk with the ambition of developing industry on the West Coast.

Yet another veteran of both the war and the '49 tour was Bob Stuart from Canterbury. He captained the All Blacks on the 1953–54 tour to the UK, which included Brian Fitzpatrick (Sean's father). While he finished up playing after that trip, Bob quickly moved into coaching and was an adviser to the All Blacks for the monumental 1956 series against the Springboks. He also had a younger brother named Kevin, who played one test against the Wallabies in 1955.

By now, one of the most famous brothers in All Blacks history had made his debut. Ian Clarke began his career in Bob Stuart's side to the UK, and would be joined in '56 by brother Don. While their story is explained in greater detail with a chapter of their own, they aren't the only brothers named Clarke to play for the All Blacks. First five Adrian Clarke from Auckland also appears on the team sheets of the late '50s, probably leading many over the years to presume (erroneously) that he was one of the famous family from the Waikato. His last test was the 13–0 beating the

All Blacks took on the first test of the 1960 tour to South Africa.

By the time Adrian's actual brother Phil made the All Blacks in 1967, all the Clarkes that he was and wasn't related to had retired. Unfortunately, Phil's All Blacks career is one of extreme brevity. He came out of nowhere to make the team; as a member of the RNZAF he'd been posted around the country and was with Marlborough at the time, impressing in a trial match that catapulted him onto the hastily arranged tour to the UK. Phil Clarke only played the first four matches before getting injured, meaning that he watched on as the All Blacks swept through and won all their test matches.

Super Sid ended up spending the next decade feeding the scrum for the All Blacks, and scoring 164 points in 86 games including 29 tests.

One of the players Phil would have seen begin an illustrious career with the All Blacks was halfback Sid Going from North Auckland. Super Sid ended up spending the next decade feeding the scrum for the All Blacks, and scoring 164 points in 86 games including 29 tests. He's regarded as one of the best in that position for any team, ever. His brother Ken, a fullback, was selected for the 1974 tour of Ireland. He was 32 at the time, making him one of the oldest debutants in All Blacks history.

Ken spent the tour as the back-up to Joe Karam, who these days has managed the rare feat of not having his status as a former All Black be the first thing people associate him with (Marc Ellis may well be the only other one). The Going brothers played together in only one game for the All Blacks, against Connacht, and after the tour Ken wasn't picked for the national side again.

He shouldn't feel like he was alone in that, though. The 1970s saw an awful lot of players picked for the All Blacks in often comparatively short tours and only a few games. Lyn Jaffray, a first five from Otago, somehow managed to be on the edge of selection so often that he played seven tests in seven years. His debut was outside Sid Going in 1972 against a touring Australian team so bad it became known as the 'Woeful Wallabies', but then he didn't play again until the 1975 'Water Polo' test at Eden Park against Scotland (look it up on YouTube and you'll see why it got its soggy name).

While Lyn went on the 1976 tour of South Africa, his brother Merv was picked for another All Blacks tour later that year to Argentina. This was a bit of a throwback to the days of when two separate sides would play different tours, and also to when games that should have been tests aren't counted. Merv played two games against a full Argentine side, which in this day and age the All Blacks do every year, but they weren't recorded as tests because the Pumas weren't a full member of the International Rugby Board at the time.

Lyn was the starting first five in one of the All Blacks' most famous losses, to Munster in 1978. Also on that tour was another first five from North Auckland, Eddie Dunn. He made a name for himself on the tour by kicking a last-minute, winning dropped goal against the Barbarians in Cardiff in the last game of the Grand Slam tour of the UK—which doesn't fit the narrative of free-flowing games involving the Barbarians. His All Blacks career ended by 1981, replaced for the upcoming series against the Springboks. Two years later his brother Ian spent a season in the All Blacks as a first five as well, winning a series against the British Lions.

Another player of great promise on the '76 tour to Argentina was Waikato first five Murray Taylor. His performances convinced many that he might finally be the one to stop the revolving door of men in the 10 jersey, but unfortunately he broke his leg playing club rugby the following year. The injury was so severe it kept him off the field for two years. However, he managed to get himself back into the All Blacks frame and make his test debut against France in 1979. He ended up competing with Eddie Dunn on the tour to Europe at the end of the year, and by 1980 was picked for the two-test Bledisloe Cup series.

The All Blacks scored one of their greatest tries ever in the second test in Brisbane, started and finished by Hika Reid over an 80-metre movement of perfect running and passing.

It's here where the most often replayed footage of Murray Taylor's career can be found. The All Blacks scored one of their greatest tries ever in the second test in Brisbane, started and finished by Hika Reid over an 80-metre movement of perfect running and passing. Murray was the last, crucial link, stepping and drawing the last defenders before offloading for his hooker to dive over. It was also the last test he played, and he retired at the end of the next season because of complications with his broken leg. Two years later, his younger brother made sure the family name was back on the team sheet.

Warwick Taylor had moved south to play for Canterbury by the time he was picked for the All Blacks in 1983. His career spanned a series victory over the British Lions, the Cavaliers tour and a World Cup victory, as well as playing in the epic 1985 Ranfurly Shield game between Canterbury and Auckland. Just like Murray, he was alongside one of the Dunn brothers for his debut, this time Ian. Warwick's career lasted until 1988, ending on the All Blacks tour to Australia.

LEFT: Don 'The Boot' Clarke lines up yet another shot at goal for the All Blacks. **PHOTOSPORT**

RIGHT: New Zealand in a simpler time. Ian (left) and Don Clarke: farmers during the week, All Blacks on Saturday afternoon. **PHOTOSPORT**

DON AND IAN CLARKE

WAIKATO STADIUM IN HAMILTON SITS just to the north-west of the town. Its large light towers are visible as you drive in from Auckland, making it easy to find your way there for a Super Rugby game featuring the Chiefs. The Ranfurly Shield has made the stadium its home an awful lot in the past few decades. The Super Rugby trophy also spent time there in 2012 and 2013.

It used to be known as Rugby Park, another pragmatic New Zealand name presumably inspired by the folks that named the North and South Islands. Today the seats are all a uniform orange, with a lush green bank behind the southern goal line a nod to its illustrious past as a venue of some of the most notable moments in rugby history.

When you walk up the staircase inside the western stand, which houses the corporate and media facilities, you can see the stadium's history in all its glory. Pictures of famous Waikato rugby moments line the walls of the long climb to the top of the stand: Waikato fans from the post-war period adorned with yellow, black and red ribbons; Shield glory; and Reverend George Armstrong passionately appealing to a line of helmeted policemen during the 1981 Springbok tour pitch invasion, which ultimately forced the cancellation of the match against Waikato.

Wind the clock back 25 years, though, and the Springboks received a very different reception at Rugby Park. To say this was a big day in New Zealand rugby history is selling it about a mile short—the 1956 tour was the most anticipated sporting event in New Zealand history until perhaps the 2011 Rugby World Cup final. Even then, no one had to queue up outside Eden Park overnight to watch the All Blacks scrape home against France.

For all that the New Zealand rugby public likes to think that the All Blacks have been the most dominant team in the world since forever, there's a distinct chunk of time between 1937 and 1956 when they most definitely weren't.

The Springboks had come to New Zealand in '37 and famously won a test series by outsmarting, out-tackling and outplaying the All Blacks. World War II intervened and meant they didn't meet each other again until 1949, when the All Blacks suffered their worst year ever: a 4–0 series loss in South Africa, coupled with the bizarre decision to play the Wallabies at home at the same time with a different All Blacks team. It meant that on 3 September of that year, the All Blacks reached the distinction of being the only test side to lose twice on the same day, with the touring side going down 9–3 in Durban and the home side getting on the wrong side of an 11–6 scoreline against the Wallabies in Wellington.

Given how much analysis and soul-searching goes into a rare loss these days—when losses happen at a rate of one to two a year—you can imagine what New Zealand was like after the All Blacks lost six tests in one season. Especially considering that seven years needed to pass before the All Blacks could gain any sort of retribution.

It was about then that the image of rugby being New Zealand's national obsession was cemented. It was an era of tough, low-scoring, conservative games. The old saying goes that 'the forwards win you the game, the backs decide by how much'; in reality the first part was right but the latter probably came down to the goal kicker. Generally, test matches and important provincial games would follow a pattern of one team getting out to a two-score lead, then grimly hanging on no matter how much time was left.

Don and Ian Clarke provided both of those components. They would have both strapped on heavy leather boots and strung the laces under the soles. Fields would have regularly turned into bogs, including their home track of Rugby Park.

Test matches and important provincial games would follow a pattern of one team getting out to a two-score lead, then grimly hanging on no matter how much time was left.

The Clarkes were a Waikato farming family, which in those days meant a rugby family. Parents Alec and Ann Clarke moved around, but finally settled at a dairy farm in Hoe-O-Tainui, north of Morrinsville. They had five sons: Ian, Douglas, Donald, Graeme and Brian. All grew up to be big boys, then big men. Don's primary-school class photo shows him comically dwarfing the other children, a good head and shoulders above everyone else except for the teacher.

One of the family's paddocks had a set of goalposts, as well as a carefully prepared cricket pitch for the brothers to hone their skills on.

All five of the Clarke brothers played for Kereone RFC. Don made his debut for Waikato at age 17, in 1951. He played fullback, and quickly gained a reputation for being an accurate goal kicker after Waikato's Ranfurly Shield victory over North Auckland that season. What was more notable, though, was his size. By now he stood 6'2" and weighed around 110 kg. This made him regularly the biggest player on any side he played for, including the All Blacks. Ian had first played for Waikato the same year, but was in the more traditional big man's position of prop. He was a powerful scrummager and a natural leader.

This was well before the era of a National Provincial Championship, when unions would get together and organise a slate of games for the season depending on how strong they respectively were. Waikato were still a young union, having only been formed in 1921.

The Clarkes grew up in the heart of post-war New Zealand. This was a time when the country seemed to bask in prosperity; the baby-boomer generation were raised on quarter-acre sections, and their parents who lived through the Depression and World War II could relax, smoke inside and drive home from the pub after the six o'clock swill.

Hamilton isn't exactly a towering metropolis now, let alone in the 1950s, but it was the centre of the universe as far as footy went that day.

Now both Don and Ian found themselves lining up against the Boks on 9 June 1956. The D-Day of the biggest rugby invasion the country had ever seen.

Hamilton isn't exactly a towering metropolis now, let alone in the 1950s, but it was the centre of the universe as far as footy went that day. It was centred right on the cut-up paddock of Rugby Park, a far cry from the pool tables that get played on in this century. On both sides, players wore heavy leather boots that reached right up around the ankles—supposedly to give support but probably greatly increasing the risk of lower-leg injury.

The Clarke brothers and probably most of the rest of both teams would have walked out, clanking their heavy metal sprigs along the concrete corridors of Rugby Park, with short hairstyles pretty much identical to what Sonny Bill Williams made popular over half a century later. Side parts looked good then, too, but generally didn't last long in the muddy conditions.

Liniment pervaded the atmosphere, filling up nostrils and heightening the tension that the first game of the tour already carried in abundance.

The crowd would have arrived early, driving in from around the region. Perhaps a few, too, who had ventured south from Auckland to get a glimpse of the almighty Springboks. Around 31,000 were jammed into the stands and embankments, impatiently sitting through a string of curtain-raisers.

Long-sleeved jerseys, the Waikato ones without their emblem of a cocked right arm brandishing a mere. Not much different to the ones the Brownlies would have pulled on after they came back from their war. Plenty of veterans of both conflicts watched on, joined by a few grandfathers too old to have even enlisted in the first one. There were plenty more who would have stayed home to help New Zealand's role as an imperial farming outpost during World War II, tending herds and baling hay in the Waikato region while the war raged across the water in the Pacific. Plenty of smashing back quart bottles and hip flasks, chain-smoking and finding places to piss.

There were nine games in five weeks before the first test in Dunedin for the Springboks to get through, these days an outrageous ask for a side to play. Tough assignments coming up too, with the likes of Auckland and Wellington given the task of softening up the enemy so the All Blacks could get their revenge that was 19 years in the making.

Ian Clarke had been a part of the brewing storm that was about to unleash. He earned his first test cap in 1953, and went to the UK on a tour that is often brought up as the last time that Wales ever beat the All Blacks. That day at Cardiff Arms Park was Ian's test debut. Although they beat the other home unions in low-scoring matches, the All Blacks also dropped a test to France for the first time. Given the standards that the team is held to, the 1953–54 tour isn't regarded as one to remember.

It lasted across the entire northern winter, with the loss to France coming on 27 February 1954. Contrast that to today, when the All Blacks' obligations last until November, and February is when Super Rugby kicks off. The upside-down nature of the fixtures meant that no home tests were played throughout the 1954 season; in fact the All Blacks didn't play again until August of the following year.

The oldest of the Clarke brothers did come out of it with his reputation sufficiently intact, though. Once the All Blacks resumed playing in 1955, Ian was named captain and led the side to a 2–1 series victory over the Wallabies. Not only that, he had a position switch to number 8, due to some encouraging games there during the previous tour as a fill-in, and also because selectors back then were inclined to make utterly baffling, reactionary choices. The flip-side of that occurred the next season, when Ian was replaced as skipper for the all-important Springbok tour. He wasn't even named captain for the Waikato side that would face them first up.

However, the years after Don's breakout season as a 17-year-old kicking prodigy hadn't quite gone according to plan. He spent the next year out with injury, only to come back and find himself the second-string fullback. He missed another entire season in 1955, and it seemed like his legacy would be as a footnote in Ranfurly Shield history. But he fought his way back into the side, having a great deal of faith placed in him by Waikato and future All Blacks coach Dick Everest.

The ground was so full that the crowd sat only a few feet away from the touch- and dead-ball lines. All of them were on their feet when Malcolm MacDonald scored Waikato's first try after only three minutes.

The sound of the sprigs on the concrete and the dark surrounds of the changing rooms would have finally given way to green grass and sunshine as the Springboks and Waikato got onto the park. This was it. Time for the tour to begin, and the younger of the Clarkes to start a feverish conversation about how the All Blacks would need both brothers in the side to win the upcoming series.

The ground was so full that the crowd sat only a few feet away from the touch- and dead-ball lines. All of them were on their feet when Malcolm MacDonald scored Waikato's first try after only three minutes. After 20 minutes, winger Jack Bullick got his face rearranged and had to leave the field. Bear in mind this was 1956 and you weren't allowed replacements, so number 8 Rex Pickering shifted out to cover the wing. That left Ian's forward pack down a man for over half the game, but of course scrums back then were more of a loosely arranged alley-fight than the overly engineered game killers they are now. So while it was still a challenge, the Springboks couldn't rely on simply winning penalties off set piece.

While Don's first few shots at goal had gone astray, including an ambitious attempt from his own half, he imposed himself on the game in the most dramatic fashion. After receiving a pass, he lined up and snapped a dropped goal from 40 metres out. That in itself is pretty impressive, but Don delivered the strike with his left foot.

Waikato shot out to a 14–0 lead at half-time, which is the same as being up by about 35 these days. Don had kicked the goals that mattered, because the Boks came storming back in the second half to make the score 14–10. Against all pre-match predictions, the undermanned home side hung on and won.

The kids ran onto the field, people could barely believe what they'd seen and the players retired to the sheds that no doubt still reeked of liniment. On to the after-match, held in the Waikato Rugby Union's rooms. Full of booze and smoke, where the visitors honoured their vanquishers by presenting them with a mounted springbok head. It's still sitting on the wall of the supporters' club at Waikato Stadium, taking pride of place alongside the faded photos and old memorabilia.

The Springboks made their way unbeaten through the rest of their lead-up games, with the first test taking place at Carisbrook in Dunedin. It was a brutal affair, with the All Blacks getting home 10–6 courtesy of a Ron Jarden intercept try. The next test was even more of a dour slugfest, but this time the Springboks hit back with an 8–3 win at Athletic Park.

To say the alarm bells went off is an understatement. It was more like a nationwide civil defence emergency. It might seem hard to imagine now, given just how tightly controlled test squads are, but the All Blacks selectors saw fit to make seven changes to the team. No one was safe, with jazz-loving skipper Pat Vincent being replaced by the Clarkes' Kereone and Waikato teammate Ponty Reid.

Kevin Skinner was coaxed out of retirement to add some much-needed intimidation to the All Blacks front row. The former New Zealand heavyweight champion went on to famously punch out Springbok prop Chris Koch, then swapped sides of the scrum with Ian to do the same to Jaap Bekker.

> **To say the alarm bells went off is an understatement. It was more like a nationwide civil defence emergency . . . the All Blacks selectors saw fit to make seven changes to the team.**

But the headline news was that the big man from Waikato was coming in to lend his right boot to the proceedings. The call-up for Don Clarke came at what could probably be described as the All Blacks' biggest test to date; losses in Christchurch and Auckland could have changed the course of rugby history. Given just how much was riding on the series, and how much national prestige was at stake, the dent from an even more prolonged drought against the Boks may well have altered the entire perception of the All Blacks.

There are pictures of the fans in those days, the hardy souls in a black-and-white world waiting outside the gates of the grounds. They would camp there, night after night until game day, waiting to get into the terraces. This was New Zealand in the 1950s, a place where you'd think nothing of sleeping on a concrete footpath simply for a view of a game of rugby. If you were an exceptionally committed cheapskate, or knew one, you could get a look at the game from a rickety homemade grandstand. Many sprang up in the neighbouring properties banked up alongside the test venues, and in Dunedin plenty simply sat on the hill surrounding Carisbrook.

Lancaster Park, now a barren wasteland after the 2011 earthquake, was the venue for Don's debut. The crowd rolled in, clad in tweed jackets and hats, again a good five to ten thousand more than the ground was supposed to fit.

The barrel-chested Clarke brothers took to the field; by now Ian was an old hand, but Don's demeanour suggested this was no big deal for him either. The fullback, by now 22, had gained a reputation as a confident, almost arrogant guy—although that presumption should be tempered with the fact that New Zealand society was so awfully straight-laced it's likely any showing of confidence would be regarded as highly suspicious.

It wasn't long into the game that he got his first chance to show off why he was known as 'The Boot'. From 41 metres back, a shade in from the sideline, Don hammered home the first points of his All Blacks career: 3–0. Then 6–0. Then 11–0 after Morrie Dixon crossed in the corner. All of them tough shots made to look easy. If it seemed like a rerun of the tour opener, the Springboks made it an almost carbon copy by coming back and scoring two converted tries in the second half.

There was a crowd of somewhere around 55,000 at Lancaster Park that day, but flickering black-and-white images, triumphant music and a voice-over artist thoroughly concerned with sounding as British as possible is how everyone who wasn't actually there got to see it. In some cases they waited days before the newsreel footage came to movie theatres around the country, with many presumably more interested in that than the main feature.

In a perfect world, they would have seen Don have the last say with a game-sealing kick to complete a heroic debut. However, no one was complaining when the All Blacks crossed for two tries in the last few minutes to blow the score out to a comfortable 17–10.

While the finish and scoreline belied the conservative nature of the era, the main talking point was how Don Clarke had blasted the All Blacks into an unlosable series position. The last test at Eden Park drew the biggest crowd of the tour—61,240—indeed an attendance that still stands as the highest to ever watch a game of anything in New Zealand.

The eventual 11–5 win is remembered both for Peter Jones' runaway try and for his foul-mouthed post-match utterances, both of which say a lot about the New Zealand of the time. The piece of brilliant athleticism and determination defined everything that the All Blacks stood for, followed by a national clutch of the pearls when someone dared to say the word 'bugger' into a microphone.

Don 'The Boot' Clarke had gone from being a local to a national hero. It wasn't long before he became an icon; as an established member of the All Blacks he racked up an incredible (even by today's standards) 163 points from 13 games on the 1957 tour to Australia.

'The crowd will tell you . . . listen . . . it's a goal!'

If you're not old enough to remember Winston McCarthy, that was the most famous piece of rugby commentary until Keith

Quinn's quasi-orgasmic meltdown over Jonah Lomu at the 1995 World Cup semi-final.

McCarthy was the main commentator for the National Broadcasting Service, broadcasting all of the All Blacks' games to living-room radio sets throughout the 1950s. That phrase, instructing everyone sitting at home to continue what they'd been doing for the whole game anyway, was what McCarthy would invariably say whenever someone was taking a shot at goal.

In fact, McCarthy belting out his trademark call while Clarke stroked another penalty or conversion through the uprights basically became a soundtrack to that period of New Zealand history. But it is most synonymous with one game, in a series where Don Clarke delivered his most famous moments. Of course, just how that game is perceived depends on whether you buy into the concept that it's important for the All Blacks to be the more entertaining team.

There's an editorial in the *1959 Rugby Almanack of New Zealand*, bemoaning the often teeth-pullingly boring way some rugby had been played in the previous season:

> It may, however, not be out of place to record our
> disappointment at the purely negative and defensive tactics
> so often adopted by some unions, and even New Zealand,
> when it is considered a victory must be attained at all costs.
> We cannot but feel that such exhibitions do the game harm.
> Surely the end is not so all-important as that.

It's hard to find a more prescient statement about what was about to happen in the first test of the '59 season against the British Lions, in terms of public reaction. Don was going to find himself right at the centre of one of the most talked-about games in All Blacks history.

He banged over six penalties in the test, at the time a world record. The Lions scored four tries, and the headline afterwards read 'Lions 17 Clarke 18'. So began a long and mythologised debate about how this was the most shameful All Blacks win ever.

The man in charge that day wasn't only a Kiwi—referee Alan Fleury was a Dunedin local controlling a game in front of many people who knew him personally. The four tries he awarded were highly entertaining. Welshman Malcolm Price bagged a double, Englishman Peter Jackson and Irishman Tony O'Reilly got one each.

It was all set up to be a triumph of running rugby over the dour, kick-happy game of the All Blacks, except Don was nailing his shots from everywhere, most importantly the one that gave the All Blacks the lead with two minutes to go.

It's worth mentioning that the stats indicate Fleury gave out a whopping 20 penalties to each side in that test—half that number would be considered a whistle-happy performance in this day and age. It wasn't his fault that the tourists couldn't kick their goals. However, it meant little to the Dunedin crowd. They turned on him and the All Blacks for what they perceived to be an unfair result. Legend has it they were chanting 'Red, red, red!' as the clock ticked down, and booed when Clarke's winner went over.

Yes, that all seems a little unbelievable. The All Blacks being so boring that their own crowd wanted the other team to win? The British being the bastion of entertaining, enterprising rugby? A ref who could probably have walked back home after the game?

For his part, Don rubbished any criticism of the way in which the test was won, saying:

The Lions infringed, were penalised, and I was in sufficiently good form to kick the goals . . . certainly I felt no misgivings on my part. People said afterwards, 'I wish you'd missed that last one.' I was delighted to kick it and win it. To have done anything else—to have deliberately missed as they seemed to suggest—would not have been rugby to me. And just think what another section of the public would have said if I had thrown the match away!

The next test in Wellington saw Don again play the part of the hero, except this time the All Blacks won in a manner that better befitted their reputation. Down 8–6 with time running out, the fullback hit the line hard as the All Blacks desperately searched for a winner. He latched onto a pass in midfield and launched his gigantic frame over the goal line, then knocked over the conversion for good measure to make it an 11–8 win. It was one of only two tries he scored in test matches.

It was around this time that Don started to arouse some serious interest from British rugby league clubs. The money on offer was enough to get him considering a code switch, but ultimately secure employment in New Zealand and the likelihood of an undesirable position switch to loose forward meant it never went further than that.

The next year the Clarke brothers travelled with the rest of the All Blacks to South Africa, by now a simmering hotbed of tension after 12 years of apartheid and centuries of oppression. This was the series that changed the view of sporting relations with the Springboks, given that the NZRFU once again caved to the 'whites only' selection policy that the South Africans demanded. This was the same policy that helped South Africa win in 1949, which makes the All Blacks' willingness to accept it even more baffling.

Don's big boot couldn't land anything as the Boks blanked the All Blacks 13–0 in the first test at Ellis Park. It remains the last time the All Blacks failed to score a point in a loss (they drew 0–0 against Scotland four years later).

Don's big boot couldn't land anything as the Boks blanked the All Blacks 13–0 in the first test at Ellis Park. It remains the last time the All Blacks failed to score a point in a loss.

The All Blacks had fallen into a trap they really should've known about, anyway. Remembering the 1949 tour, a chat to any locals or even a cursory glance at a map would have given them some clue about Johannesburg's altitude difference, but their lack of preparation meant that the team was hit hard by the thin air. Ian recalled in a 1965 interview:

> It was very, very hard training. When you first get up there you don't sort of notice it, but after a couple of days it hits you hard. You feel like sleeping a couple of hours every afternoon. When we got up there we did not look the same team. There was no question about it: our players looked very dead. Especially in the second half, as things got on a bit, some of our chaps were barely out of a walk. They [South Africa] really played well, that was not a good game for New Zealand.

They pulled back the second test in Cape Town 11–3, but it was in the drawn third test that both Clarke brothers played starring roles in the dramatic final act of the game.

Just like in New Zealand, Free State Stadium was about 10,000 people fuller than it should have been. In another anachronism that conveniently shoehorns Ian into the story, touch judges were provided by non-playing reserves from either team—so the discarded prop took his place on the sideline with a flag.

The score stood at a predictable-looking 11–3 to the Springboks as time was running out. Don stepped up and got the All Blacks within striking distance with a 60-metre penalty. Then, off a hopeful kick ahead, All Blacks winger Frank McMullen crossed just inside the corner flag. Again it was up to Don, balancing the ball on the rock-hard South African turf. A stadium full of 60,000 home fans willed him to miss.

Don slammed home the sideline conversion, earning a draw and keeping the series alive. Ian, wearing his All Blacks blazer, put the flag up before it had even gone through the sticks.

All Blacks captain Wilson Whineray was back on halfway, and nervously glanced up to see Don striding back before the ball had even cleared the posts. He remembered talking to his fullback:

> I said, 'Good lord I didn't watch it, I wasn't up for that . . .
> but I thought you would have shown more interest.' He said,
> 'I didn't need to. As soon as I struck it, I knew.'

Whineray, who was later knighted for his services to rugby and business and therefore a man who can be counted on to say the right things, can also be credited with one of the best descriptions of Don in general:

On the field he was like a huge energy force behind you. Even when he missed a kick, it could have a devastating effect on the opposition.

Of course, the performance was essentially for nought as it didn't eventuate into an elusive win in South Africa for the All Blacks— they lost the last test 8–3 in Port Elizabeth and the series 2–1. McMullen and Don were denied the chance to be the heroes by a controversial double-movement call in the dying stages. Ian remembered that the day 'was not a good one for rugby'.

There was a very strong gusty wind blowing. Often a wind like that is worse than straight wet or mud. Terry Lineen and Don did a lot of drop kicks, but none of them went over. There was a lot of time wasted with these, because the ball went dead and it took a while to get it back into play. We didn't make good use of the wind that day.

One year later and it seemed like the All Blacks hadn't learned from that experience either. Athletic Park, Wellington was the venue for the second test against France. The ground had just opened the unbelievably exposed Millard Stand, a poorly designed double-decker stand that felt dangerous even on a nice day. Unfortunately, 5 August 1961 was not one of those.

Athletic Park sat at the apex of Berhampore Hill in the south of the city. If you were to head in a straight line south (where the wind was coming from that day), the next land mass you'd hit is Antarctica. If it was a bad day for rugby in Port Elizabeth the previous season, the conditions for the French test were pretty much apocalyptic: a 130 km/h wind cursed the playing field for the entire 80 minutes, making it difficult for the players to even hear each other speak. The French looked on track to take a memorable 3–0 win, after an incredible effort by Jean Dupuy to run a dropped All Blacks pass back into the teeth of the gale for an unconverted try.

After teeing the ball up, Don Clarke sent a shot almost parallel to the 22-metre line and let the wind do the rest.

The All Blacks staggeringly failed to use the wind advantage at all in the second half, until Kel Tremain scored a sloppy try in the corner as time was running out. The score was 3–3 with a kick to come, on a ground where Don hadn't exactly impressed in his previous outings. What happened next has been told countless times, but the best way to describe it is in the words of the man himself.

'That kick was an absolute fluke,' Don said in his biography. 'No one could have judged that hurricane.'

After teeing the ball up, Don Clarke sent a shot almost parallel to the 22-metre line and let the wind do the rest. End over end, it veered inwards and rocketed through the uprights, giving the All Blacks an improbable and somewhat undeserved win.

That year, 1961, the other Clarke brothers made their way into the family legend when all five of them represented Waikato in a game against Thames Valley. Graeme, Doug and Brian all pulled on the Mooloo jersey. In fact the other three Clarkes managed to forge respectable rep careers of their own. Graeme had 72 games for Waikato, Brian 70 and Doug 43. The 11–8 win over Thames Valley is the only time all five appeared together in a first-class game, but having four of them at once happened more than a few times.

It's worth mentioning that this could well have been a story about three Clarke brothers. Doug was widely considered good enough to get an All Blacks call-up, too; however, according to Colin Meads: 'He was one of the unlucky ones who never got the big break at the top level but having two brothers there already made it awkward.' It's a good thing that kind of thinking had changed by the time the Barrett family came along.

By the time the next All Blacks tour of the UK and Canada rolled around in 1963, Ian was 32 and Don 29. The tour was to be their last; Don's persistent knee trouble had already started to sideline him from provincial games. It didn't stop him from playing an outstanding cricket season, though. Thanks to all the time spent playing his brothers on their homemade pitch, he had been a regular fixture in the Northern Districts side since 1956. In the 1962–63 summer he had picked up 20 wickets to help them win the Plunket Shield for the first time, including an outstanding bowling performance against Central Districts that saw him finish with figures of 8/37.

The Clarke brothers' story does have one last twist in the tail. That farewell tour, which saw the All Blacks grind out drab wins against Ireland, Wales and England, as well as the draw against Scotland, concluded the British leg with a match against the Barbarians. Ian was invited to play for the Baabaas for the game at Cardiff Arms Park, and found himself lining up against Don for the first time ever in a first-class game.

For all the kicks that Don had put through the uprights in his career, the last notable act of the boot from a Clarke brother ended up coming from Ian. In keeping with the mythological nature of their careers, it was through an act of scoring that's been obsolete for over 50 years now.

A goal from a mark says exactly what it is in the title, but actually scoring one was pretty difficult. Catching a kick on the full for a mark was allowed anywhere in the field of play before 1977, and if one was claimed close enough to the posts then the player could drop kick a goal if he wished. The state of most fields, coupled with the fact that most rugby players couldn't drop kick to save their lives, made them incredibly rare. Ironically, Don had recorded one just the previous season against England at Eden Park from his own side of halfway.

> **For all the kicks that Don had put through the uprights in his career, the last notable act of the boot from a Clarke brother ended up coming from Ian.**

Perhaps it was a case of 'anything you can do, I can do better', or even that the two had conspired to make it happen. The latter theory certainly holds a bit of water upon review of the grainy footage, as it genuinely looks like Don searched out his brother when he went to restart play. His kick floated straight into Ian's hands, who then immediately signalled to the referee that he'd take a shot at goal. He didn't muck around, taking the ball back before launching a drop kick from the All Blacks' 10-metre line that went straight through the posts and put the Barbarians into the lead, 3–0.

Ian and the Barbarians may well have been dreaming of an unlikely upset, but any notion of that evaporated quickly. The All

Blacks decided to start playing and ran in eight tries to win 36–3, the most famous of all being Wilson Whineray's suave dummy and nonchalant plant under the sticks to finish proceedings while the Cardiff crowd chanted his name.

That was Ian's last international match of note. Don's farewell to the All Blacks came later in 1964 against the Wallabies at Athletic Park. It wasn't a happy day in the capital, like when he scored the winning try against the Lions or somehow kicked the winning goal against France. The All Blacks lost 20–5, in a stunningly poor display that would stand as the Wallabies' biggest win over them for another 35 years. For all the heroic deeds he'd accomplished, the biggest All Blacks superstar of the time was denied a fitting fairy-tale finish.

Ian had played 252 first-class games, including 24 tests for the All Blacks. Don had 226 games, 31 tests and 781 points for the All Blacks. His 207 test points set a world record, which was predicted never to be broken. Cynics have suggested that the first All Black who got close, Allan Hewson in the early '80s, was dropped in no small part due to the powers-that-be not wanting him to break Don Clarke's record.

If true, it was a particularly futile move due to the game changing rapidly in both scoring frequency and tests played. It was eventually eclipsed by Grant Fox after only his twelfth test. The record is now held by Dan Carter's mammoth career total of 1598 test points. In a nice bit of symmetry, both Don Clarke and Dan Carter's most talked-about performances came against the British Lions, though they are 46 years apart and remembered in quite different ways.

Both Clarkes moved into post-All Blacks life, but never strayed far from the game that defined their lives. With rugby being amateur, both already had careers they could now commit fully to. Ian had a dairy farm in Morrinsville. Don was a salesman with Rothmans, surely a sign of the times that a legendary All Black could transition into selling tobacco. He fell foul of the NZRFU in 1965 for daring to suggest that test matches should be shown live on television, and was well ahead of his time in advocating for tactical substitutions.

There must have been something about the 1960 tour to South Africa that struck a chord with Don, as he moved there to live in 1977 with his wife, Patsy, and three children. He started a tree-felling business in Johannesburg.

Ian continued to run his farm, and became a referee. He went on to become vice-president of the NZRFU, eventually rising to president in 1993. He advocated long and hard to get the All Blacks to play a test match in Hamilton. His vision became a reality when they thrashed Argentina at Rugby Park 62–10 in 1997. The next day, 29 June, Ian was out on the farm when he collapsed and died. He was 66.

That same day, Don was involved in a serious traffic accident when a truck smashed into the side of his ute in Johannesburg. He recovered from his injuries, only to develop melanoma just a few years later. He was an old-school man with an old-school disregard towards protecting himself against the sun.

Don made one last emotional journey back to New Zealand in 2001, to attend a vast reunion of his All Blacks teammates. Some 70 of them had assembled at Eden Park to raise funds for his fight against cancer, an event that left the legendarily confident Don 'bewildered and overwhelmed'. He held on for one more year, before passing away on 29 December 2002.

The Clarke brothers forged a vital part of the perceived era of innocence in New Zealand rugby. The time when it seemed like rugby really was all that mattered; when people would go to the movies just to see newsreel footage of All Blacks tests; and stadiums were packed out well beyond their capacity. These days, it's a completely different world—Rugby Park is now Waikato Stadium, a far cry from the rickety stands and embankments that surrounded Don and Ian playing against the Springboks in 1956.

On the staircase of the grandstand, alongside the afore-mentioned images of yesteryear, there they are in the team photo of the famous 1956 side that vanquished the Springboks. A ground that used to be a bunch of planks fashioned into bench seats, with a chopped-up paddock as a playing field. Now it's a clean, plastic and concrete building. The surface is immaculate, and the staff and supporters honour those who played their part in creating the rugby history of the province. If you ask anyone old enough at a Waikato or Chiefs game about the old days, it won't be long before they mention the Clarke brothers and what they did out on that field.

They haven't forgotten them. They never will.

The raw aggression of rugby in the 1960s—Colin (centre) and Stan Meads (far left) compete for lineout ball against the Lions in 1966. PHOTOSPORT/PETER BUSH

COLIN AND
STAN MEADS

THERE'S ONE MAN WHO CAN get into any game of rugby in New Zealand, whenever he likes. Peter Bush is in his nineties now, but still proudly owns the only 'golden bib' that New Zealand Rugby has ever given out. He is the longest-serving photographer to cover the game in New Zealand.

His images date as far back as 1949. While you can go on YouTube and watch the footage of test matches from back then, the degraded quality, cheesy backing music and fact that the camera is miles away at the top of a grandstand doesn't do it justice. It's the still image, shot by a man who can get close enough to hear the crack of taut sinews colliding, smell the sweat and liniment, and tread the same grass that's being churned up by 30 pairs of boots.

Here you can gaze at the emotion, the despair, the triumph of a black-and-white era. Maybe Bush's most famous picture is that of the second test of the 1966 series between the All Blacks and British Lions at Lancaster Park. Shot from the sideline, it shows the immediate aftermath of a lineout won cleanly by the home side. It shows a collection of some of the greatest men to ever pull on the black jersey.

The field is cut to bits, long grass curling over the top of the men's boots. Mud cakes their jerseys and skin. Behind them, a packed grandstand of people, with many more down on the ground itself, part of a 55,000-strong crowd there to see the next chapter in an already 20-game-long tour. The All Blacks had already handed the Lions two test losses; this one would be the third in an eventual series clean sweep.

Some of the main reasons for the one-sided nature of the series are right there in the photo. At the back stands Waka Nathan, then Kel Tremain, Ken Gray and Bruce McLeod. Legendary names of All Blacks history.

In the middle stands one man, holding the ball. His thumb grips the top while his massive fingers curl underneath the leather oval like it was made for children. He's crouched over, but still somehow seems far bigger than everyone else.

The Lions' Irish flanker, Noel Murphy, in between Nathan and Tremain, watches on with a look of almost weariness on his face. He knows what's coming next, because over the last few weeks he's experienced just why playing the All Blacks at home is probably the toughest assignment for any foreign rugby player.

The man with the ball is, of course, Colin Meads. Ready to pass it off to his halfback, or turn around and hurl his frame into the waiting den of Lions defenders. The rest of the All Blacks have the same expression on their faces, mouths half-open in anticipation. Next to Colin is his brother, Stan, arms outstretched to offer some protection.

If you'd never seen any of them before and had to guess which two are related, you'd probably assume that Tremain or Gray was a brother of the man holding the ball. They both have the same sweat-soaked shock of dark hair. Stan stands out like a beacon with a blond short-back-and-sides.

While the Clarke brothers' story is full of heroics of an entertaining nature—oversized blokes playing in the wrong position, kicks from halfway, a potentially jacked-up goal from a mark—this tale, while covering much of the same time period, is very different. Don and Ian Clarke were almost always smiling, handsome men with their hair spic and span. Colin and Stan Meads were the brute force of the All Blacks, earning a string of superlatives that are synonymous with their legendary surname.

Tough. Uncompromising. Ruthless.

The values that came to represent the All Blacks, so obvious in Bush's famous photo. That was in the mid-'60s though, on the eve of big changes in New Zealand and the world. The Clarkes finished their careers just as the last baby boomers were born, bringing down the curtain on an age of attachment to what was left of the British Empire. The long career of Colin meant that he bridged the gap between this idyllic part of New Zealand's growth and its slow drift to the nation we have today.

Colin and Stan Meads were the brute force of the All Blacks, earning a string of superlatives that are synonymous with their legendary surname.

But there they stand at the lineout, frozen in time as evidence of what so many people in this country regarded, indeed many still do: what it means to be an All Black.

This series ended up being Stanley Meads' last in a black jersey. His brother would go on to carve out a 14-year career, but both of their stories begin back in Te Kuiti. They were born and raised in the heart of the King Country; Colin was the elder brother by two years, having been born in 1936. He was named after his grandfather, the ominously titled Colin Brutus Meads.

By the time they were teenagers, the Meads boys were spending any spare time working on the family farm.

Farming, like rugby, was a tough proposition back in those days. Scrub clearing was done almost entirely by hand, and Vere Meads expected that his sons would do the work. Christmas and rugby were the only occasions that would see the brothers get out of the paddocks. Of course, all this farm work made the already big brothers fit, strong and in the sort of shape that would send them both on a path to a black jersey.

Colin attended Te Kuiti High School, making the first XV by the time he was 14. Later that year, he decided he'd had enough of school and left by mutual agreement with the headmaster. Of course, it being 1950, Colin was told: 'Certainly you're not worth anything in here. If you're going to leave when you're 15, you might as well leave now. We'll be doing you a favour and ourselves a favour.'

Colin and Stan were both tall, so naturally played lock. They partnered up for the Waitete club, then the King Country provincial side. Colin's first provincial game, against the then South Auckland Counties in 1955, isn't remembered for the sort of hard tackling and commitment to winning notable in the rest of his career, though. The 19-year-old found himself at first receiver in the opposition 22, and for some reason kicked a wobbly dropped goal. Stan made his debut two years later, but kept things more traditional by concentrating on lineouts and scrums.

The brothers had to trial for the King Country team, which sometimes meant playing against each other. Even at that early stage, Colin had developed the sort of rough on-field temperament that would characterise his career. When they did clash, though, Stan gave as good as he got. The brothers found out that while family bonds were no barrier to their relentless will to win on the field, after the match they had a much higher power to answer to: mother Ida. Stan recalled of one match:

> We got real nasty with one another. I remember coming home on the Monday morning and our mum, who was a very quiet lady, she lined us up at the breakfast table and gave us a real wind-up. She said 'I'll bang your heads together if you do that again.' So we thought when Mum gets into it we better back off.

However, being on the same side together was a different story.

The Meads brothers were part of a geographically large union, but one with a comparatively tiny playing base. While they lagged behind the likes of Auckland, Waikato and Canterbury in numbers, they made up for it in physicality and commitment.

'Some players with big names would come in to play King Country, and the poor buggers would go home with their tails between their legs. Honestly, they'd wonder what had hit them,' Stan said.

Stan wasn't hesitant at all in acknowledging his brother's greater prowess for the game.

> I never felt hacked off by the attention he got, have never felt I lived in his shadow and it's irritated me when people have said I was concerned about that. There was no real sibling rivalry as far as I was concerned. Of course we were competitive . . . but that is common enough to be expected.

Colin's promising junior form meant he was picked for a New Zealand Colts side that toured, of all places, Sri Lanka. It was on a New Zealand Under-23 tour to Japan where his endearing nickname of 'Pinetree' was created. He made his debut for the All Blacks in 1957, one season after the team beat the Springboks and became the unofficial champions of the world. It only took one season for him to become an established member of the team; however, he was dropped for the test where Don Clarke kicked the All Blacks past the Lions in 1959. He then played a big role on the heartbreaking tour to South Africa the next year (see the Clarke brothers' story for more on this). By the time his brother was called up to the All Blacks in 1961, Colin had played 39 games for the national team.

By then, Colin's famous attitude towards playing the game had become well known.

> I'm the first guy to try my opposition out. If I come across a fellow who's going to let me get a moral advantage over him I'll carry on doing it. It's not for any personal satisfaction or gain. It's for the team's sake. I'm conscious of when it's been done to me and move quickly to overcome it. If these activities are causing trouble then you call it quits. I'm no bloody angel.

The Meads brothers first played together in an All Blacks jersey in 1961, against France. Don and Ian Clarke lined up at prop and fullback, marking the first occasion that two sets of brothers had played for the All Blacks in a test. By chance, brothers André and Guy Boniface were opposing them in the French team. A tremendously important occasion for the family, Stan said it felt natural to have his brother next to him on the field.

We'd played together so often for Waitete and King Country that we sort of knew instinctively what the other was going to do. I think we complemented each other quite well. He was more robust than me, no doubt about that, but I was a better jumper whereas Colin wasn't really. He operated closer to the front of the lineout where you could get involved in play differently.

You could easily interpret that last part as saying that's where his brother liked to do the majority of his notorious off-the-ball hits and other dirty work.

'We never worried about scrums. We just fell into them, we had such a long history of locking scrums together. Stan was a natural, a real athlete,' said Colin.

While the story of the Meads brothers training by running up and down a hill with a sheep under each arm is regarded as a fun exaggeration of both rural life and rugby obsession in New Zealand, there is a fair element of truth to it.

The close proximity in which the brothers lived on the family farm, coupled with the landscape they inhabited, meant they could train together almost constantly. High-intensity, aerobic work. Competing against one another as to who could run the farthest and fastest, lift the heaviest. They ran the roads around the area relentlessly. Shearing. Fencing. While the story of the Meads brothers training by running up and down a hill with a sheep under each arm is regarded as a fun exaggeration of both rural life and rugby obsession in New Zealand, there is a fair element of truth to it.

There is one ovine-related story that is 100 per cent true, however. Stan's 1959 season was ruined by an injury caused by a ram butting his knee against a fence post.

In all, the Meads brothers played 11 tests together. They toured the UK in 1963–64, in which the All Blacks famously lost a match to Welsh club Newport in the early stages of the tour, but then went on to win the rest of their games apart from a 0–0 draw with Scotland.

But the tour did actually take another toll on the Meads brothers. Stan had played in the test-match win against Ireland at number 8, but became stricken with illness and missed 16 games.

Another highly anticipated Springbok tour of New Zealand came around in 1965. By now Colin was rightfully feared as the hardest man in world rugby, and was relishing the chance to dish out some revenge on the South Africans who had triumphed five years earlier. Unfortunately for the Boks, they had hit easily the lowest point in their history to date—earlier that year they'd lost tests to Ireland and Scotland, then two to the Wallabies on the way to New Zealand. It wasn't going to get any better for them once they arrived, getting thumped by Wellington in the second tour match. It was almost a relief that they only lost the first test by 6–3 in Wellington.

The All Blacks blanked them 13–0 in the next test at Carisbrook, and it looked as though the series would be a whitewash, like the year before against the Lions. The game was notable for being the site of maybe the only humorous on-field picture of Colin Meads ever taken. After the final whistle, Springbok centre John

Gainsford couldn't help himself and grabbed a handful of mud from the sodden ground. He crept up behind Meads and shoved it in his face, while a nearby photographer captured the moment.

'I chased him all the way to the dressing room,' Colin said in 2016's *Behind the Silver Fern*. 'I had a beer with him. He was laughing his head off.'

The next season saw the Lions tour, and lose the series in which Bush snapped his famous photo of the Meads brothers taking control of that lineout at Lancaster Park. Both men were at the peak of their powers, and played every minute of the 4–0 series win over the hapless British.

But this is where the on-field story ends for Stan. There was a tour scheduled for South Africa for the 1967 season that he was desperate to go on. According to Colin, Stan would have been playing on the 1960 tour, had it not been for injury. By now, though, the problem of apartheid had become a full-blown issue. The South African refusal to allow Māori players into the country caused the NZRFU, under pressure from the government, to call off the tour and hastily rearrange a replacement trip to the UK and France.

Stan had dealt with a lot of injuries in his career, plus the debilitating effects of getting sick while away in the UK for all those months. He was clearly thinking about looking after his farm and family when he pulled the pin on his rep rugby time at the end of the 1966 season.

Colin was probably wishing he'd pulled out of the tour too, because when it reached Edinburgh for another test against Scotland, he thought his career was finished as well. Up until then, the tour had been a breeze against four home unions still probably hurting from the previous year's Lions tour, and the test results had been wins against England, Wales and France. It would have included Ireland too, but there was a foot-and-mouth disease outbreak on the UK mainland, which meant that leg of the tour was cancelled.

The test against Scotland was on the way to being another regulation win, with the All Blacks up 14–3 with only a few minutes to go. The ball found its way to the deck. Scottish first five Davie Chisholm instinctively went to grab it. Meads instinctively went to kick it.

He recounted in his biography that he kicked the ball into Chisholm's body. It didn't help that Scottish hooker Frank Laidlaw immediately yelled, 'Did you see that, ref? The dirty bastard!' That description was more or less how British rugby folk viewed Meads anyway, given that he'd spent the last decade laying waste to everyone they'd sent his way. Irish referee Kevin Kelleher blew his whistle, and pointed to the changing rooms. Meads recalled the send-off in his autobiography:

> To this day I am positive he did not see what had happened.
> I am just as sure it was the commotion Frank Laidlaw was
> making that made his mind up for him. He ordered me off.
> I was shocked, couldn't believe it. My mind sort of tumbled.
> I took a couple of paces away, stopped and half-turned back,
> thinking 'he can't mean it'.

It was no use. Meads left the park despite the protests of captain Brian Lochore, and immediately presumed his career was finished. He was the second man to ever be sent off in a rugby test, after fellow All Black Cyril Brownlie 42 years previously. It would be another 50 years before Sonny Bill Williams would be the next All Black to get the same treatment. Colin thought it was all over, that this incident would spell the end of his time in a black jersey. However, those feelings didn't translate into an outburst of dramatic prose. Years later, his daughter Shelley revealed that he had written a diary while away on the tour—the entry for that day was simply: 'Sent off, got drunk'.

Of course, it was by no means the end of Colin Meads on a rugby field. Far from it. He was too valuable a part of the All Blacks to be discarded over simply doing what he'd been picked to do. And while he probably didn't deserve to get sent off in 1967, his most infamous act of on-field aggression came a year later at Athletic Park when he injured Wallaby halfback Ken Catchpole.

Years later, his daughter Shelley revealed that he had written a diary while away on the tour— the entry for that day was simply: 'Sent off, got drunk'.

One of Catchpole's legs was trapped in a ruck, so Meads took hold of the other one and wrenched it hard. The muscles in his groin were torn from his pelvis, and the story goes that it prematurely ended his career at age 28. Meads himself rubbished the claims, saying that Catchpole was back playing only a few months later at an invitational match in Tonga and was going to retire anyway.

That's one famous injury, but the one that is mostly associated with Colin Meads is one he suffered himself. If it had happened to the Brownlies in the 1920s, a hefty dose of scepticism would exist, not least from the medical profession. But it did happen, and is now probably the most telling part of the Meads legacy.

Rugby is a sport that likes to humble-brag about just how tough it is these days. Constant comparisons to soccer and American football are prevalent on social media, to the point of being slightly embarrassing. There are countless, often cringeworthy, memes and videos vaunting rugby's perceived courage and superiority in terms of what a player will endure in order to win, or at least give 100 per cent to their team. It is, of course, mostly nonsense.

But this sort of reputation had to be earned somewhere, and it is tales of injuries such as what happened to Colin Meads against Eastern Transvaal in 1970 that cemented the notion that rugby is indeed the hardest sport of all. Injuries were, like now, a big part of the game. How they were dealt with was an entirely different matter, however. Fractured bones regularly cause players to sit out for months these days, and a clean break will likely end an entire season.

Meads had his arm broken 10 minutes into the All Blacks' sixth match of the 1970 tour to South Africa. It was from a kick by one of the home players, who has never been identified. Meads believed it was a pulled nerve, and played on for the rest of the game.

Even by the old-school standards of toughness and complete disregard for one's own health, this is staggering. This wasn't just a hairline fracture from a bit of incidental contact. It was a targeted act to deprive the All Blacks of one of their best players for the test series—and it worked, for the first two tests anyway. Just how it happened, though, is best told by the people who were there.

As per usual with rugby tours, the provincial games before the test series were ostensibly to provide the visiting team with some warm-up time, but also for the home union to surreptitiously injure key players. It wasn't at all uncommon; New Zealand teams weren't averse to a bit of 'softening up' themselves. So it came as no shock to Brian Lochore when the boots came flying thick and fast early in the Eastern Transvaal fixture.

'Clearly they weren't worried at all about who was on the ground when they came at you. It was pretty physical,' he said in a 2017 interview.

'Our response was that we're going to give them everything we've got. We weren't going to back off,' said halfback Sid Going.

Still, there were some who were better at dealing with the onslaught than others. The average size of a back in a game of this era was generally no more than 80 kg, so if any of them were caught at the bottom of a ruck they could expect a decent working over. The All Blacks forwards had to protect them from the consequences of a big Eastern Transvaal forward having a psychotic penchant for tap-dancing on the opposition.

'We were getting the hell knocked out of us. There were boots flying everywhere at the bottom of the rucks,' said first five Earle Kirton. 'I went down on the ball, he [Meads] said "I'll cover you up". Then I heard a "whack". He had his arms around me, hugging me almost to cover me up, and someone had booted his arm.'

The two men got up. In typical laconic style, this was the exchange of words:

Meads: 'I can't feel my fingers.'

Kirton: 'Aw shit Pinetree, you haven't broken it, have you?'

Meads: 'Well I don't know.'

Kirton: 'I wouldn't worry about it now. See how it goes and if it doesn't come right, we're in trouble.'

Of course, it turns out Kirton's original prognosis was spot on. It was a clean break of Colin's radius, one of the two bones that connect your elbow to your hand. A bad injury in any circumstance, one that would generally require at least a month in a cast, then around six months to a year to rehabilitate. Colin Meads simply jogged to the next ruck and continued the game.

There's a code of honour among the men who played rugby back then, a bit like the one that exists among career criminals. With no footage of the game in existence (live TV coverage of rugby in New Zealand was still six years away), no one has ever been accused of committing the act that broke Colin Meads' arm. From their accounts, it's obvious that Going and Lochore have no interest in being snitches—Lochore claimed he 'didn't see the incident', while Going said 'it probably was deliberate, but there's no way of knowing'.

There's a code of honour among the men who played rugby back then, a bit like the one that exists among career criminals.

With all due respect to the great halfback, it's hard to accidentally break someone's arm. That sort of damage requires some premeditation, and the sight of one of the most important All Blacks lying there prone would have been too tasty to ignore for one of the opposition. Meads may as well have painted a bullseye on his forearm.

He wasn't alone, either. Lochore ended the game with a broken nose, and 11 more All Blacks picked up injuries in the game. Ten more minutes passed before Meads went to the sideline for help, but he was told by a South African doctor (the All Blacks did not have an official team doctor with them) that it must be a pinched nerve. He headed back out onto the field and finished the game. It seems almost superfluous to note that the All Blacks ended up winning quite comfortably, 24–3.

Substitutions had only just recently been made legal, so he could have been replaced. But nobody, not even Meads himself, knew how serious the injury was. Lochore says that if he had, there was no doubt that he would have had Meads swapped out so he could get some treatment.

But, Lochore continues, 'We didn't want him to go off, he was a very important part of our side. Pinetree never wanted to go off.'

'In the heat of the moment you don't have too much time to think about it, because you're worried about making sure you're performing well yourself. For the sake of the team he battled on and thought "she'll be right". He was so tough,' said Kirton.

'They were sent out there to make sure they knocked a few guys out. You expect that, it's part of the South African way. You accept that, they're mad keen on their rugby and they love it,' Kirton continued, reflecting the spirit of the times, in which the violence meted out that day was simply par for the course.

It was somewhat telling that his former teammates had no qualms with his eventual decision to play on.

'Some said he shouldn't. It was really down to the man and the fact that he was a wonderful attribute to the team. They feared him and they respected him, the South Africans, so he needed to take the field for that reason alone,' said Lochore.

The most legendary part of the story was after full-time, when the doctor presumably had a proper look at his arm and confirmed it was indeed broken. Meads simply growled, 'At least we won the bloody game.'

This may as well have been interpreted as a benchmark for his teammates, because Colin Meads' hard-nosed attitude towards ignoring even the most insane pain thresholds was expected of the rest of the All Blacks, too. Prop Keith Murdoch, later the subject of an infamous chapter of his own in All Blacks history, came down with appendicitis before the last test against the Springboks. Meads apparently told him he 'could not not play', and that settled the matter. It's worth noting that the most severe side effect of a ruptured appendix is an extremely painful death, but Murdoch duly waited until the end of the tour and promptly had it removed.

That's how they rolled in 1970.

Pinetree's injury was given seven weeks to come right, which is well short of the recommended healing time for a break of that severity. Meads shed the cast before the third test against the Springboks in Port Elizabeth, and covered it up with a leather guard. While the series stood at 1–1, his presence in the last two tests eventually didn't make the difference. The last two were lost to the Springboks, and with that went Meads' final chance to win a test series in South Africa.

Back home, the landscape regarding the All Blacks playing the Springboks had changed quite a bit from when Colin and Stan had lined up against them in 1965. While there was definitely a level of protest on that tour and the one in 1960, the straw that broke the camel's back in terms of pushing the issue into the general consciousness of New Zealand was the exclusion of Māori players from touring. Going, as well as superstar Bryan Williams, had to gain a ridiculous exemption to even set foot in apartheid South Africa. They were known as 'honorary whites', a term lifted directly from Nazi Germany's wartime alliance with the Empire of Japan. However, while Meads' long playing career was now entering its twilight, 1970 was not the last time he'd be involved in a tour to South Africa. And the next one would prove to be much more problematic.

His last season of test rugby was in 1971. Meads was now 35, and the recently broken arm was another addition to the litany of serious knocks he'd taken over the past couple of decades playing top-flight footy. One more series to go, against the British Lions at home. He'd already been a part of two victories against the home countries: on the field for Don Clarke's heroics in 1959 and bullying the 1966 Lions out of the country with their tails between their legs.

The signs that the 1971 Lions side was going to be a far more daunting proposition were evident in the lead-up to the first test. They blew past Waikato, Wellington and Canterbury and showed that they had the makings of a team that could take the All Blacks on up front and control play through their two world-class halves, Barry John and Gareth Edwards. However, British rugby was still seen as nowhere near the sort of threat as the Springboks.

In contrast, though, the All Blacks were in a state of flux. Brian Lochore's retirement after the Springbok series loss the year before had left the side without a skipper. They were big boots to fill—he finished with a record of 18 wins and three losses, the latter all occurring on the South African tour. The All Blacks selectors chose Meads to take the reins, which seemed a logical choice given that he held the record for the most tests played and by now completely epitomised everything about the national side. However, there were six new caps in the All Blacks for the first test.

The Lions duly shocked the All Blacks in the first test, winning 9–3 in something that resembled an 80-minute knock-on-a-thon. For all the talk in the years since regarding the Lions' exciting backline, a quick glance at the footage of this game will probably have modern viewers scratching their heads as to where that presumption came from. This was an arm wrestle, up the middle of a very muddy Carisbrook. It should've been a place for Meads to stand up and dish out his own brand of home-town justice on the assorted English, Welsh, Scots and Irish forwards.

But it never came. All of a sudden, the All Blacks were on the back foot. Although the next test was won 22–12 in Christchurch, the situation ushered in another piece of All Blacks legend—the famous call-up out of retirement for Brian Lochore for the third test in Wellington. Lochore left a brief note on the kitchen table for his wife letting her know he'd be away for the weekend. Sadly, he ought not to have bothered: the Lions ground out a 13–3 win and control of the series.

The last test at Eden Park, which the All Blacks had to win to save face, ended up being Colin Meads' last. That the heroics in the game came from a player so far removed from what Meads stood for was rather poetic—J. P. R. Williams, a flashy Welsh fullback with long hair and thick sideburns, snapping a dropped goal out of the blue just like Meads did in his provincial debut. Unlike Meads, though, the Welshman showboated all the way back to the halfway line. It proved to be the crucial score in a game that finished 14–14. The series had been lost, 2–1.

That test has now become arguably the greatest day in the Lions' history. It has somewhat overshadowed the fact that it would be the last time Colin Meads would ever pull on an All Blacks jersey, but he had no intention of retiring when the full-time whistle blew.

It was a motoring accident that finally spelled the end of his All Blacks career. In the summer following the Lions tour, Meads was heading home and rolled his Land Rover off the road. The damage done meant he missed the entirety of the 1972 season. By the time he regained his health, he was too old to reclaim his spot in the team. He kept playing for King Country until 1975, then hung up the boots for good.

He'd pledged to his wife, Verna, that he'd take a good break from rugby, but that promise didn't last long. He became coach of King Country in 1976.

Stan once said about Colin that 'nothing gave him more satisfaction than beating the Springboks'.

Getting sent off against Scotland and being responsible for Catchpole's injury (probably a fair few others, too) are forgivable given the way rugby was played in the old days. However, the Cavaliers tour in 1986 is a little bit different.

Stan once said about Colin that 'nothing gave him more satisfaction than beating the Springboks'. Indeed Stan himself hung up his boots when he realised that his dream of touring South Africa was unlikely to ever happen. So it's easy to understand Colin's desire to keep the greatest rivalry in rugby going, even though sporting contact with South Africa had been in the gun for the previous two decades.

Meads was the coach of the rebel Cavaliers team, which is ironic considering that one of the greatest All Blacks of all time played such a pivotal role in almost the entire team turning their backs on the jersey. Note the word 'almost', because it's important for the somewhat inadvertent role it had in a key moment in World Cup history. The team were banned once they returned home, with many having played their last-ever games for the All Blacks. Meads himself was sacked as an All Blacks selector. The effect snowballed into the inaugural World Cup in 1987, where the two players who refused to join Meads with the Cavaliers, John Kirwan and David Kirk, ended up being the tournament's top try scorer and the winning captain respectively.

The Cavaliers tour was a disaster on and off the field. The team had to sneak out of—then back into—the country, and rumours that they'd been paid for their treachery came thick and fast. They lost the series against the Springboks 3–1. In an ugly bit of symmetry with Meads' career, captain Andy Dalton had his jaw broken in a midweek game against Northern Transvaal, ruling him out of the rest of the tour and ending his season. It's probably accurate to presume that Meads would have reminded Dalton that a broken bone hadn't stopped him playing a test series in South Africa.

Stan also had a hand in coaching, although his stint was far less controversial, and more befitting the sort of rural setting the brothers grew up in. He was called in to take over the running of the King Country team mid-season in 1995, and guided them to a crucial upset win over Canterbury to keep them in the NPC first division that year.

Colin Meads has almost indisputably become the greatest All Black of all time. However, thanks to a decision he made in 1990, there are more than a few English rugby folk who don't even rate him as the best lock to play for King Country. While he wasn't directly responsible for bringing Martin Johnson to the province as a 19-year-old, he certainly did help to shape him into the uncompromising player that would go on to captain England and win a World Cup.

Local club coach John Albert was the one who had the idea to send an open letter to members of the English schoolboys' team, asking them to head to New Zealand to hone their skills. Colin agreed to mentor anyone who answered the call for help.

By that time, the King Country union definitely needed the boost. The local forestry industry had been in decline, stripping the area of a key pool of players. Meads originally thought it was a 'crazy idea', arguing that the New Zealand talent pool should be deep enough. But Albert convinced him and the letter was sent.

Rugby by that stage was a different game aesthetically from the one Meads played, but rucking, skulduggery and outright violence were definitely still very much a part of it.

The 19-year-old Johnson arrived sight unseen, having paid for his own plane ticket, and was given accommodation at Albert's family home. Meads set about fulfilling his obligation as mentor. All his years of aggression, determination and rule-bending were passed on to the impressionable Englishman. Rugby by that stage was a different game aesthetically from the one Meads played, but rucking, skulduggery and outright violence were definitely still very much a part of it.

The lesson was absorbed, refined and channelled by Johnson, who was quickly ushered into the King Country side for the National Provincial Championship. A strong season there meant he was eventually picked, with a strong endorsement from Colin, for the New Zealand Under-21 side.

He even played in New Zealand's most traditional fixture, against Australia in Sydney. Marking him for the Australian Under-21 side was another future icon, John Eales.

The prodigy of Colin Meads was suddenly on the path to becoming an All Black. He wouldn't have been the first Englishman to do so; indeed there had been two in the previous decade. Jamie Salmon and John Gallagher had both pulled on the black jersey, with the former swapping his for an England one (this was back in the days of switching test allegiance at will) and the latter eventually going on an ill-fated journey to rugby league. Gallagher in particular left with his legacy ensured, winning a World Cup and being regarded as one of the best fullbacks to ever play for the All Blacks.

What would New Zealand make of a young Englishman taking over a position that was so ingrained in the national identity?

But this was different. Johnson was a forward, a lock even. The biggest part of the engine room and a spot that the Meads brothers themselves had mythologised. What would New Zealand make of a young Englishman taking over a position that was so ingrained in the national identity?

We'll never know. Instead of taking the path to the black jersey, Johnson packed up and went home. He left behind what may well have been an anchoring role in a New Zealand provincial side, a career in Super Rugby and glory with the All Blacks. A long-standing rivalry with Eales. The path he chose, though, would bring English rugby as close as they have come to having a Meads of their own.

Johnson spent his entire career at Leicester, playing an incredible 362 games. He played 84 tests for England, ending in a monumental World Cup win as captain, and a series win for the British Lions in South Africa.

Could he have got there without his stint in New Zealand under the tutelage of Meads on the Te Kuiti turf? Of course, given that his attitude and focus were lauded during his time at King Country. Albert said of him:

> He was very comfortable in who he was but he also knew what he wanted to be. I found myself fascinated by the strength of his commitment to the cause on the rugby pitch.
> For a youngster, he made quite an impact.

But it will always be one of the great 'what-ifs' of rugby. The next-gen Meads 2.0, trained in the same heartland as the man himself. If nothing else, it'd be a fantastic movie.

Many of Colin Meads' influences have become integral to the way the All Blacks run. Much to the chagrin of many a journalist over the years, the media is treated with utmost suspicion. The roots of mistrust lie with some unsurprisingly poor advice Colin received at the start of his test career from the NZRFU, whose secretary told him that if he wanted to stay in the All Blacks, 'never speak to a reporter—and especially don't speak to Terry McLean'.

Meads said, 'I was so scared of being seen with him. He came up at breakfast one day in Australia, and asked if he could join me. I mumbled "yeah", but then put my knife and fork down on my half-finished bacon and eggs, and without a word to him, rushed out of the room.'

He was never short of a word while he was All Blacks manager, though. After an uncharacteristically poor 22–15 loss to France in 1995, Meads assembled the entire team and staff, giving them a blow-up for the ages. One by one, the management were verbally ejected from the room by Meads—even coach Laurie Mains—until only the players were left. Whatever was said next clearly worked. The All Blacks won the next test 37–12.

There are constant comparisons between players from yesteryear and today. Most are a waste of time, but it is interesting to ponder just how the Meads brothers would go if they'd been born 50 years later. Both stood 6'4" (193 cm), so they both had the stature to make a Super Rugby side as a blindside at least. But what if they'd been on a modern diet and weight programme instead of clearing scrub and general farm work? Also, with the advent of cameras catching every slight bit of foul play, how would Colin have imposed himself on a game?

After an uncharacteristically poor 22–15 loss to France in 1995, Meads assembled the entire team and staff, giving them a blow-up for the ages.

Stan, now in his eighties, is in no doubt that they could still run modern players off the park.

'Colin and I would have hacked it today, I've no doubt about that. We'd eat most of them as far as fitness goes.'

There is a statue of Colin Meads in Te Kuiti now. It was unveiled in June 2017, during the landmark British & Irish Lions tour that swept the country like the ones he'd played in back in 1959, 1966 and 1971. In a replay of Colin's last test, the All Blacks and Lions ended up playing out a draw at Eden Park. Travelling British fans made the pilgrimage to the heart of the King Country, as well as Lions manager John Spencer, who had opposed Meads on the 1971 tour as a player.

By then, Colin Meads (now Sir) was battling pancreatic cancer. The country was bracing itself for the mighty Pinetree to fall. The passing of the greatest All Black came on the weekend of an All Blacks test win over the Wallabies, on 20 August 2017.

A bit of New Zealand died with Colin Meads. His career bridged a change from New Zealand being a provincial British backwater to a nation that had done away with the death penalty, switched to decimal currency, and committed troops to Vietnam.

His 134 games for the All Blacks remained a record until it was overtaken by Richie McCaw in 2014.

Stan gave his brother's eulogy at the funeral in Te Kuiti, which was attended by thousands including a number of former All Blacks, as well as being live-streamed throughout the country. In probably the biggest shock of the entire proceedings, he revealed that their mother had taught Colin how to knit and that is how he'd spent some of his spare time.

Maybe the most pertinent statement that Colin made during his lifetime about Stan was this: 'We knew each other's games, we had a bond.'

The last word by Stan, at Colin's funeral, summed up just what that bond meant.

'My brother has always been a good bugger.'

LEFT: Gary (centre) and AJ Whetton (far right), along with Sean Fitzpatrick, exhausted after emptying their tanks in another All Blacks test win. Team manager John Sturgeon looks on. **PHOTOSPORT/PETER BUSH**

RIGHT: AJ would always follow just behind Gary whenever the team ran onto the field. **PHOTOSPORT**

GARY AND AJ WHETTON

IT'S 18 AUGUST 1990. Athletic Park is ready for the last match of that year's Bledisloe Cup series, which has already been won by the All Blacks with two regulation victories in Christchurch and Auckland. The last one brought up 50 unbeaten matches in a row for the All Blacks, over the course of the last three years. Despite the typically disgusting Wellington weather, this should be another one.

The Wallabies have the makings of a good side. But the talk on everyone's lips isn't about how they may well pose a threat at the second edition of the Rugby World Cup the next year, but rather who will be leading the All Blacks out onto the field that day. Or, more accurately, who won't be. It's been a tumultuous time for the national team—now Gary Whetton is about to find out that he can add becoming captain to a decent list of achievements that haven't gone quite according to script.

He's been handed the reins in place of Wayne 'Buck' Shelford, the extremely popular number 8 from North Harbour. Shelford's axing has caused a sensation around the country. He's been unbeaten while captaining the side, brought mana and strength to the All Blacks haka, and famously played on after having his scrotum torn open in a test against France in 1986. The event will cause one of the most enduring traditions in New Zealand, three simple words that can transcend sports and connect Kiwis the world over. Already, in the stands around Athletic Park, makeshift banners that are little more than spray-painted bedsheets are bearing the resonant phrase: Bring Back Buck.

Gary Whetton stands in the tunnel, at the head of the line of players. It's his third test in charge; in the first at Lancaster Park his twin brother AJ stood behind him—a show of support that required Grant Fox's permission to supplant his traditional spot for when the teams take the field. The Whetton brothers have played 27 games alongside each other for the All Blacks and are established members of the side that three years previously became the first official Rugby World Cup champions.

The first test match, as far as captaincy debuts go, was more or less perfect for Gary Whetton. The All Blacks won 21–6 at Lancaster Park and then followed that up with a 27–17 victory at Eden Park. But the shock of having an All Blacks captain replaced, especially one with such a powerful reputation, still had people questioning what coach Alex 'Grizz' Wyllie was doing putting Gary Whetton in charge.

Gary and Alan 'AJ' Whetton are the only twins to have played test rugby for New Zealand. They were part of one of the greatest All Blacks sides ever, and undoubtedly the greatest provincial side ever.

At the end of the afternoon in Wellington, the volume on those murmurs had been turned up considerably. The All Blacks' unbeaten streak was gone, and the loss would set off a chain of events that would see the World Cup relinquished to that very same opponent a year later. Sounds like the end of a downbeat story? Well, it's not; in fact it's far from it. Gary and Alan 'AJ' Whetton are the only twins to have played test rugby for New Zealand. They were part of one of the greatest All Blacks sides ever, and undoubtedly the greatest provincial side ever. While the focus these days is on the way the Whettons finished their careers and the fractured state of the All Blacks in that time period, the previous decade saw a series of highs and lows of which both twins were right at the forefront.

While the Brownlie, Clarke and Meads brothers grew up in the heartland of New Zealand on their family farms, the Whettons were city boys. They hailed from Auckland city, the historically powerful province that had produced its fair share of All Blacks. Wilson Whineray, who captained Don and Ian, then Colin and Stan, was the epitome of the Auckland All Black—a tough, big leader who was an eloquent speaker and held an air of sophistication that only a city-dwelling New Zealander would have possessed in the 1960s.

The Whetton brothers were born in 1959, so would have grown up hearing tales of Meads charging down the pitch against the Springboks and Lions. Just like Colin and Stan, they would grow up to be big boys; however, when they were packed off to Auckland Grammar, rugby wasn't at the forefront of their minds. Gary was worried about the size of the older boys playing rugby at Grammar and chanced his arm at soccer instead. Alan was a self-described nerd who took piano lessons and wore horn-rimmed reading glasses.

By the time they had made it through to seventh form (year 13 in today's language) the twins' growth spurts had kicked in and applying it on a rugby field became a no-brainer. Auckland

Grammar had a long history of dominating the local college first XV competition, and the twins were expected to continue that tradition. It helped that the team was stacked with the likes of John Drake and Grant Fox.

That year, 1977, saw AJ play a starring role. The former nerd had transitioned into a skilful lock forward and his form saw him picked for the Auckland age-grade rep side. Meanwhile, Gary had the size but also had a habit of being a lazy trainer that saw him fail to distinguish himself until after the boys had left school and were competing for the Grammar Old Boys club. Gary put his change in attitude down to a trip on the Outward Bound outdoor education course.

The change was dramatic. All of a sudden he was in the Auckland Colts side, destined for the big time. In 1979, AJ joined him, having switched to the loose forwards. By now, the gap that had existed between the two had completely closed—they were entrenched in the same club and rep side. It only seemed a matter of time before they'd get their call-ups to the full Auckland provincial team.

Gary and AJ aren't identical twins. In fact, it's pretty easy to tell them apart given that Gary is a bit taller and darker in complexion. By this early stage of his career, Gary had grown his trademark moustache, removing any doubt as to which Whetton brother was which.

Gary found himself pulling on the blue-and-white hooped jersey in 1980, as a 20-year-old. But any chance of a slow and steady rise to prominence went out the window the next year. It was going to be a year that changed not only his life, but pretty much everyone else's around him as well. Just mentioning the year 1981 conjures up serious emotions among many New Zealanders, whether they're rugby fans or not. Gary Whetton was about to be thrown into the heart of the biggest civil disturbance the country had seen that century.

Like the Clarke and Meads brothers, the Whetton twins' story has a healthy chunk of South Africa attached to it. What had been a gigantic, all-encompassing act of national pride in 1956, then steadily morphed into a source of serious protest by 1970, now found itself the number-one moral divide of 1981. Five years previously, the All Blacks had effectively ruined the 1976 Montreal Olympics by touring South Africa. The tour led to a boycott by members of the African National Congress, which is why when you watch footage of John Walker winning a gold medal in the 1500 metres, all the athletes coming in behind him are white.

Just mentioning the year 1981 conjures up serious emotions among any New Zealanders old enough to remember it, whether they're rugby fans or not.

Once again in 1976, non-Pākehā players were designated 'honorary whites', which by then had become basically apartheid South Africa's convenient way of ensuring they'd get Japanese investment in their diamond mines. It also meant that the country could do something about keeping international sporting contact going. They'd already been banned from the Olympics, FIFA and international test cricket, but the International Rugby Board didn't have any problems with the Springboks continuing to play throughout the '70s. The only thing stopping the All Blacks from playing the Boks more often was the New Zealand government, which had signed an agreement at the Commonwealth Heads of Government meeting at Gleneagles in 1977, in which every nation agreed to suspend sporting contact with South Africa. It turned out the Gleneagles agreement wasn't worth the paper it was printed on to the new National Party government in 1978, who immediately gave the NZRFU permission to start planning for another test series. The 1981 tour of New Zealand was to go ahead, despite all signs pointing towards it being a complete calamity in the making.

Gary had helped Auckland to fifth place in the relatively new National Provincial Championship the year before. The NPC had been contested since 1976, and the traditional powerhouse hadn't yet managed to get their hands on a title. The next decade, though, would more than make up for that.

The 1981 season with Auckland had been going well for Gary, despite Auckland being a mid-table team again. He had been touted as a future All Black, but that too was something that was supposed to happen down the line. Andy Haden, perpetrator of possibly the best (or worst, depending on which side you're looking at it from) act of cheating in the history of rugby when he dived out of a lineout in a game against Wales in 1978, was an immovable part of the All Blacks locking combination. However, there was conjecture over the other spot. Graeme Higginson was the incumbent going into the first test, which was won 14–9 by the All Blacks in Christchurch, but then he was replaced by Frank Oliver for the second.

In the lead-up to that game, though, the country was quickly starting to resemble a battleground. Anti-tour protesters had successfully had the second tour game against Waikato called off, by storming the Rugby Park pitch in Hamilton before kick-off.

They were then pelted with beer bottles as police escorted them from the ground. That set the tone for the rest of the tour, with grounds being converted into fortresses surrounded by shipping crates, barbed wire and riot police.

Gary's Auckland side were on their tour of the South Island when he got word that he was in contention for the second test against the Springboks in Wellington (bear in mind this was 1981 and provincial teams still travelled mostly on trains and buses, so a trip down south would entail a few games in a row), but a call-up never eventuated for a test match that ended in a 24–12 loss to the Springboks. Gary took his exclusion reasonably well—at 21 he thought he probably wasn't ready—then after the loss the All Blacks suffered he could tell himself that he'd dodged a bullet.

A week later, though, it was a different story. The twins still lived at home with mum Ann and dad Ken. It was Ann who heard the third team announced on the radio, while Gary was still in bed asleep. He'd only had 14 games for Auckland, but now found himself starting a test match against the Springboks. In a 2018 interview with Newstalk ZB, he recalled:

> I didn't know a lot of things about anything. It was like going to war. We had the Red Squad (the police's dedicated anti-protest task force set up specifically for the tour) surrounding our hotel 24 hours a day. Protesters outside, Eden Park like a fortress.

It didn't get any calmer on game day. The All Blacks had to travel with a police escort to Eden Park at 9am on the morning of the game. If they thought that was rough, the Springboks had been secretly sleeping in the stadium for the past three days to avoid any potential blockage of their route by protesters.

The anti-tour movement had failed to stop the tour, and couldn't stop the game kicking off. Outside Eden Park, protesters turned out in their highest numbers and clashed with police.

Paradoxically, the atmosphere outside did little to alter Gary's mood once he found himself warming up.

'It was my first test, so "was this normal?" I don't know. All I wanted to do was put on my jersey and get on the field. Once you hit the field you forget about all that. You've got a job to do and you start doing it.'

However, this was anything but normal. As well as the chaos raging outside, there was going to be a light plane swooping in and around Eden Park throughout the game.

Somehow, the game got under way when Welsh referee Clive Norling blew time on, after nervously looking skyward to check on the plane that had arrived in the airspace above the ground. There were 50,000 in the crowd, and the plane would routinely drop leaflets, smoke bombs and, famously, flour bombs on the field. The All Blacks played easily their best half an hour of rugby in the whole series to start proceedings: first Stu Wilson scored a stunning try, then Gary Knight crashed over to help them to a 16–3 lead at half-time. The series, played under such incredible circumstances, looked headed the All Blacks' way in a comfortable win, and Gary was on track to have a dream debut.

He'd acquitted himself well in the lineouts against the big Springbok lock Louis Moolman. The open, running game suited his approach and he threw himself around the field. His partnership with Haden was working well as the older man could concentrate on the tight work.

Then the second half started. The plane was lowering its altitude on every pass of the ground, at one point apparently going as low as the grandstand. With all the drama happening on the streets and in the air, the actual rugby game at the centre of all the unrest was about to have an incredible climax as well.

Springbok captain Wynand Claassen put it down to the fact that the All Blacks were playing into the direction that the plane was coming from, which had made his side gun-shy in the first half because they could see its flight path and get understandably distracted. Maybe it was because the Springboks actually started playing like the team that had comfortably beaten the All Blacks the previous week. Or maybe it was because the plane's bombardier managed to hit one of the All Blacks, try scorer Knight, with a flour bomb.

With all the drama happening on the streets and in the air, the actual rugby game at the centre of all the unrest was about to have an incredible climax as well.

Whatever the reason, it ended up with winger Ray Mordt scoring three tries—the first time the All Blacks had conceded a hat-trick in their entire test history. As regulation time expired, the score stood at 22–22. Springboks first five Naas Botha missed a sideline conversion that would have given the Boks the lead, but with all the disruption, there was still an extra eight minutes of play to go.

The All Blacks needed a kickable penalty, and got one as the game finally came to a close after all that extra time. Needless to say, the Springboks were pretty unhappy with the way that it came about, which was a very dubious call involving them not being 10 metres back from a free kick. If there wasn't a gigantic protest that had been raging for weeks happening outside (by now local gangs had joined in, taking advantage of a free hit at the police), that call definitely would have been the defining moment of the series.

It seems almost comical that such a hard-fought series of brutal matches and off-field violence was finally settled by the dainty kicking style of All Blacks fullback Allan Hewson. His tiptoeing approach to the ball nonetheless connected with a 40-metre shot that sailed through the sticks and raised the flags, making the final score 25–22.

'God, what's going to happen if this misses?' ran through Gary's mind. 'You know, fear's an interesting thing. When you get to that end of it, when it's 22-all, it's come to the last seconds of a tumultuous tour that's divided the country and everything else—well, you definitely didn't want to lose.'

While a draw might have been a more poetic finish to the tour, symbolising the fact that no victory for rugby had been gained, the fact of the matter is that Gary Whetton had got his career off to a winning start. The *New Zealand Times* reporter Alex Veysey prophetically wrote in his match report:

> The All Blacks had no finer forwards than the three big men Andy Haden, Gary Knight and young newcomer Gary Whetton. For newcomer Whetton it was the beginning of a long and, I expect, distinguished international career.

The feeling amongst the Springboks was that they'd been robbed, and Moolman refused to swap jerseys with Gary afterwards.

Gary still retains some of the black-and-white attitude that many would have held about the 1981 Springbok tour when it happened, on either side. But he can also see the bigger picture.

'I was a kid growing up in New Zealand whose ambition it was to play for the All Blacks. I was given the opportunity to pull on the jersey and play our foe, the Springboks. So I have no regrets about that whatsoever. Should the tour have happened? Well that's a different matter again.'

It was done, though. Gary's baptism of fire meant that he was selected for the end-of-year tour to Romania and France. AJ, meanwhile, had been watching his twin brother's progression with great interest. He'd also made his debut for Auckland that season, but hadn't yet quite cracked it into the top XV just yet.

The next season, both of them combined to help Auckland win their first ever NPC title, under the tutelage of new coach John Hart. Once the test series rolled around, Gary was replaced by Graeme Higginson for the first couple of tests against the Wallabies. He regained his spot after the second test was lost, and played a role in a 33–18 win that locked up the Bledisloe Cup. Things were looking good for Gary, but the 1983 season would derail everything.

Gary picked up a knee injury in an invitational match in South Africa. It ended his season, which would have included a tilt against Ranfurly Shield holders Canterbury and a test series against the British Lions. However, there was a silver lining. His absence meant that AJ could get the game time he needed to establish himself in the Auckland side. AJ had been hampered somewhat by his ability to play both lock and loose forward, so he was seen as a jack of all trades. However, his time for Auckland at lock in his brother's place proved one thing: AJ was not a lock.

Hart kept him in for the long haul as a new type of blindside flanker, one who was mobile enough to get around the park but also play as an extra tight forward if needed.

This was the start of a period of domination that would define provincial rugby in the 1980s, but 1983 ended with Auckland losing both their NPC title and a much-hyped Ranfurly Shield challenge to Canterbury. The challenge ended in a 31–9 loss, but it set up the next Shield game between those two unions as an absolute blockbuster.

There was the little matter of AJ joining his brother in the All Blacks before then, though. Turns out Hart wasn't the only one he was impressing. He was called into the All Blacks for their tour of Australia, and made his debut against Queensland B. A couple of weeks later, he made his test debut against the Wallabies in Sydney by coming on as a replacement. It wasn't quite as dramatic a debut as Gary's—no planes flying over dropping flour bombs or even a stunning fightback and thrilling finish. In fact, the All Blacks lost, 16–9. AJ stayed on the bench for the next two tests, which saw the All Blacks fight back and retain the Bledisloe Cup for a 2–1 series win.

While replacements were allowed by now, AJ and the rest of the bench were only allowed on the park if someone had been injured. He understandably found it an incredibly frustrating existence.

> You're just going out there to watch as a spectator really; just one of the 45,000 people watching the game. All of a sudden—it may be 50 minutes through the game—you're asked to go on. You've been following the game and things mightn't be going well and you have to get out there and get stuck in. It takes your body 10 minutes or so to get tuned

in to what's happening. By the time you do, the game's over and you wonder where it's gone.

Provincial rugby these days is a bit of a sad sight for those who are old enough to remember just what sort of fervour it generated when the Whetton twins were in full flight for Auckland. The big stadiums would regularly have crowds of up to 40,000 for NPC games, but it was the Ranfurly Shield challenges that would fill them to capacity. Ground zero was Lancaster Park in 1985, when the Auckland side returned to make amends for the drubbing they got two years before.

Gary, AJ and the rest of the Auckland team were confronted with 52,000 Canterbury supporters and a home side that boasted the likes of Wayne Smith, Robbie Deans, Jock Hobbs and Andy Earl. However, Auckland was stacked. They had no fewer than 11 current or future All Blacks, including Grant Fox, John Kirwan, John Drake and Steve McDowell, and Hart had spent two whole years stewing over the failure of Auckland's last challenge.

What eventuated has gone down as the greatest provincial game in New Zealand history. Auckland managed to shoot out to a 24–0 lead at half-time, thanks to tries by Joe Stanley, Terry Wright, Drake and Kirwan. Canterbury coach Grizz Wyllie, who was punched in the back by an irate crowd member when he took the field to address his team, gave a famously brief half-time speech. It's been often transcribed as 'if they can score 24 points in 40 minutes, so can you'—but those words were almost definitely interspersed with some much stronger language.

The words, however terse, hit the target. Canterbury came flying back, scoring tries through Craig Green, Wayne Smith, Bruce Deans and Albert Anderson to almost snatch the game. It all came down to a bomb from Robbie Deans that landed in the Auckland in-goal area. If it had bounced the other way, maybe it would have been the greatest comeback ever. But it went dead, the cauldron of fans looked on in disbelief, and the game ended 28–23. Auckland had stopped Canterbury's Shield reign at 25 defences, which equalled Auckland's record run in the early to mid-'60s. Now, though, the Ranfurly Shield wasn't going to change hands for quite a while—Auckland would lock it up for 61 defences. In fact, the next time it moved, both Gary and AJ's playing careers had finished.

Unbelievably, the NZRFU either had collective amnesia about what had happened in 1981, or they decided to ignore the fact that South Africa was at the height of the apartheid regime. They arranged a tour to take place in 1985, despite the fact that it was almost certain to cause another mass protest. It wouldn't take much—by the mid-'80s New Zealand had a strong counter-culture movement, with protests erupting over banning nuclear weapons, Treaty of Waitangi issues and homosexual law reform. This time, though, the union would fail to have its way.

The NZRFU arranged a tour to take place in 1985, despite the fact that it was almost certain to cause another mass protest.

Two Auckland club players successfully sought a court injunction against the tour on the basis that it was at odds with the NZRFU's mission statement that they would 'foster and encourage the game of rugby'. You'd think all the barbed wire, cops and violence in '81 would have been sufficiently compelling evidence. Ultimately, it meant that the tour was cancelled, sending the All Blacks on a hastily arranged tour to Argentina instead.

In the background, though, deals were being made. It looked as though there was a way for Gary and AJ to tour South Africa after all. The now-infamous Cavaliers tour of 1986 was secretly organised, complete with Colin Meads signing on as coach and Ian Kirkpatrick as manager. It was an opportunity that the twins weren't going to pass up.

AJ went as far as declaring that he regards his start in the third match against the Springboks as his actual test debut.

'As the guys say, "You only play one first test." Well, that was it for me, really. There might have been some people at home saying it wasn't a test match. But it was to the South Africans. And it really felt like one. I'll never forget going out there with Gary and 13 other guys—just us against 70,000 and a referee. That's what it was like.'

The team, which was essentially the All Blacks playing in different jerseys, was up against it from the word go. Aside from the fact that the Cavaliers were seen as mercenaries, the Springboks were stacked with talent in the mid-'80s.

AJ Whetton: 'I'll never forget going out there with Gary and 13 other guys—just us against 70,000 and a referee. That's what it was like.'

Andy Dalton getting his jaw broken against Northern Transvaal was the most infamous incident of thuggery on the tour, but it's worth mentioning that Gary copped a shocker of an illegal hit in that game too from Bok hooker Uli Schmidt. The South African teams also benefited from the fact that the referees overlooked them blatantly lifting their jumpers in the lineouts, a move that wouldn't be made legal for another decade.

The eventual 3–1 result in their favour was an accurate reflection of the strength of the team—and unfortunately gives some weight to South African opinions that the only reason the All Blacks won the World Cup a year later is because they weren't there. The twins, along with the rest of the Cavaliers, snuck back into New Zealand. Protesters were there to greet them. The games they'd played had not been shown on New Zealand television, so no one had even seen what they'd been doing for the previous six weeks. The NZRFU banned the entire side for two test matches. Meads lost his job as an All Blacks selector.

Gary and AJ watched on as the quickly assembled 'Baby Blacks' won their first test against France, then lost the first Bledisloe Cup test of the year in Wellington. Andy Earl and Gordon Macpherson started in Gary's locking spot, while Mark Brooke-Cowden and Mike Brewer took over in the blindside and number 8 roles that AJ was looking to hold down.

Despite the side containing a number of players that would go on to have distinguished All Blacks careers, Gary's reputation saw him slot back into the All Blacks for the second test against the Wallabies. AJ got his first test start too, in a 13–12 win. The next week, though, AJ found himself dropped, then completely left out of the touring squad that went to France at the end of that year. He was a casualty of the rift that the Cavaliers tour had created. Joining him on the outer was Andy Haden, who never played for the All Blacks again.

The All Blacks, and indeed the entire game of rugby in New Zealand, needed a boost, and fast. Test attendances during the mid-'80s were falling; the political overtones of the NZRFU's decision-making process were turning people away. So the first-ever Rugby World Cup in 1987 couldn't have come at a better time. For AJ, it was about to be his break into the big time.

'I was still a spare-parts man,' said AJ, 'still to establish a permanent role in the All Blacks. Here was the opportunity for me. If I was going to make it as an international player, 1987 was the time.'

Gary scored one try in his All Blacks career, against Wales. AJ ended up with 10. Astonishingly, five of them came in the first five games of the Rugby World Cup. That's a record for an All Blacks loose forward that even Kieran Read can't match. He dotted down against Italy, Fiji, Argentina, Scotland and Wales. It's also a record for consecutive tries at a World Cup that still stands, and he would have had one in the final as well if the ball had bounced into his hands instead of Michael Jones' after a charged-down Fox dropped-goal attempt.

One of the more ironic moments in Gary's career came during the World Cup, too. During the absolute hiding the All Blacks dished out to Wales in the semi-final, he was sucker-punched by Welsh lock Huw Richards. The Welshman was in turn knocked unconscious by none other than Buck Shelford, the man who Gary would replace as captain three years later. To make matters worse for Richards, he woke up to find himself being sent off by ref Kerry Fitzgerald for starting the extremely one-sided fight.

The tournament itself, while remembered fondly by All Blacks fans, was very much the definition of humble beginnings. These days, the Rugby World Cup is a billion-dollar industry, with tickets sold months in advance and attendances making it one of the biggest international sporting events in the world. In 1987, though, some of the sponsorship deals were only getting sorted out a fortnight before the tournament began and the opening ceremony featured a local brass band. Pool-play games not involving the All Blacks or Wallabies (half the tournament was held in Australia) were sparsely attended. But the final between New Zealand and France at Eden Park has etched itself into New Zealand sporting history.

'Among the All Blacks it was as if 1986 had been forgotten . . . the tour of France, the Cavaliers, everything. No one said anything directly but it was clear that everyone wanted this to be a fresh start, a new beginning,' AJ said.

There was a massive crowd that day. Everything went according to plan against France, with the All Blacks scoring three memorable tries to Jones, David Kirk and John Kirwan.

With South Africa finally locked out in the cold until they sorted out their political system, no one other than the Wallabies came close to toppling the All Blacks as they embarked on their 50-game unbeaten run.

Gary and AJ put in massive efforts to help secure the 29–9 win. There was something symbolic about the fact that the cherubic, well-educated halfback Kirk got to lift the Webb Ellis Cup at the end, in place of the injured Andy Dalton. It showed that rugby had turned a corner in terms of its public perception after the last half-dozen tumultuous years. Kirk would retire at the end of that season, ushering in Shelford's reign as the new skipper.

For the next two seasons, the All Blacks were untouchable. Fans from that era will make a case for the late '80s being the best All Blacks side ever, and it's a strong one. With South Africa finally locked out in the cold until they sorted out their political system, no one other than the Wallabies came close to toppling the All Blacks as they embarked on their 50-game unbeaten run.

While they weren't pulling on the black jersey, the twins were part of an equally dominant Auckland side. They had now held the Ranfurly Shield for three years, and won another two NPC titles. They would add another three titles in a row. Auckland was the centre of the universe as far as rugby was concerned, and the Whetton twins were at the absolute heart and soul of its success.

Auckland were so strong in 1988 it's highly likely they would have been able to win a World Cup on their own. Seventeen games, 17 wins, 599 points for, 174 against. In a gesture that did the places they visited a world of good, Auckland put the Ranfurly Shield on the line in several away fixtures, ensuring bumper crowds in Te Kuiti, New Plymouth and Napier.

Like most rugby players, Gary Whetton had his superstitions. He would sit at the front of the bus on the left-hand side when travelling to a game, whether it was at Eden Park or anywhere else. He had a habit of picking up grass and rubbing it through his hands when he ran onto the field. He always made sure he consulted with AJ before the team ran onto the park.

AJ, meanwhile, would make sure he was behind his brother when they were in the tunnel. The twins were now an inseparable part of the rugby landscape, with Gary regarded as one of the best locks to ever play for the All Blacks. Their tour to the UK in 1989 was another reminder of just how powerful the team was—Wales and Ireland were dismembered on their home turf, and it seemed like retention of the World Cup in 1991 was a pure formality.

But before that part of the tale, we find ourselves back at Athletic Park, where this story introduced itself. Gary is now captain, and the All Blacks are looking to sweep the Wallabies in 1990. He and AJ stride out into the wet, windy conditions.

Eighty minutes later, and the Wallabies have pulled off a massive upset. Much to the chagrin of the trash-talking Sean Fitzpatrick, the crucial try for the Australians was scored by his opposite, Phil Kearns. Kearns then promptly got up and showed Fitzpatrick exactly what he thought about the All Blacks hooker's running commentary throughout the game by flipping his middle finger to him before running back to halfway. Final score: 21–9 Wallabies.

All the while, in the background, there was the constant threat of rugby league making offers that some All Blacks would find hard to resist.

The end-of-year tour to France then really showed just how much scrutiny the new captain was under. The All Blacks beat the French in both test matches, but came under fire for dropping two midweek games. Things didn't get any better when the first Bledisloe Cup test of 1991 saw them soundly beaten by the Wallabies in Sydney. Although the All Blacks pulled one back at Eden Park, the scoreline of 6–3 didn't do an awful lot to fill everyone with confidence when the team flew out to Europe to defend their World Cup title.

All the while, in the background, there was the constant

threat of rugby league making offers that some All Blacks would find hard to resist. John Gallagher and John Schuster had both left, and there were constant rumblings about Zinzan Brooke following suit. AJ had been troubled by an injury earlier in 1991 on a completely unnecessary tour to Argentina. He'd also been the perpetrator of an ugly incident in a game between Auckland and Western Samoa, getting himself banned for three weeks for stomping on Stephen Bachop.

Gary admitted that things weren't going according to plan in a pre-tournament documentary. When asked how he felt about the World Cup, he said: 'Apprehension. At this stage the team's not really fluid . . . as we get closer we'll get better.'

In his biography *Zinny: The Zinzan Brooke Story*, Zinzan described that time period as when 'the nuts and bolts of the All Blacks chassis showed signs of wear and tear. It was a sort of warning that if something was not done to put internal team matters right, the wheels would fall off—which, a few months later, at the worst possible time, they did.'

The reality was, there was a serious hierarchy issue within the team between the senior players and new boys. It had already influenced the young, confident Matthew Ridge to take up a league contract, and the effect it was having on the team was becoming untenable.

Brooke places part of the blame on Gary: 'The signs were clear but the drift persisted with no apparent concern from those who should have been doing the welding job. Young players were first perplexed and then resentful of what they took to be their second-class status. They found Gary's treatment of them offhand at best and inconsistent at worst.'

It wasn't helping that the NZRU had decided to put another

hare-brained plan into action. Grizz Wyllie and John Hart had been appointed co-coaches for the 1991 World Cup, with both having been the most high-profile provincial coaches of the previous decade. It was doomed to fail, and served mostly to elevate the tension between the Auckland and Canterbury representatives in the team that it was supposed to placate.

Then there's the fact that, by this point in time, the All Blacks were getting old. Gary and AJ were 31, and not enough work had been done to develop a team that would hit peak form by the time the World Cup rolled around. Meanwhile, the Wallabies, by accident or design, had managed to time their run to perfection.

Gary led the All Blacks to a win over England at Twickenham, which was no mean feat. But while they won the pool games and a quarter-final, they weren't by the sort of margins New Zealanders expected them to have put on Italy, USA and Canada.

Gary and AJ were 31, and not enough work had been done to develop a team that would hit peak form by the time the World Cup rolled around.

The Wallabies lay in waiting in the semi-final. They would face an All Blacks team missing Michael Jones through his commitment to not playing on Sundays, a backline without Terry Wright, and a clearly not 100 per cent fit Grant Fox. AJ didn't know it yet, but this was to be his last-ever game in an All Blacks jersey.

Just like in Sydney earlier in the year, and Wellington the year before, the Wallabies outsmarted and outplayed the All Blacks at Lansdowne Road, Dublin. It's not to say it was a complete domination, though. Gary's work at the lineout was tireless (admittedly it was pre-lifting days and winning opposition ball was a lot more common), but it couldn't stop David Campese and Tim Horan scoring two of the best tries ever against the All Blacks. Final score: 16–6. It was the most crushing defeat in years, and All Blacks fans were in shock.

One week later, it was Gary's turn to play his last match. The forgettable third-place play-off win against Scotland is where the Whetton brothers' story almost ends. The All Blacks were about to embark on several years of uncertainty and experimentation, but neither twin was going to play a part in it.

Note the word 'almost'. Like the great Colin Meads before him, there would be one more All Blacks match for Gary Whetton— just on the other side of the field.

The series was destined to be a gimmicky anomaly. But then it emerged that former captain Gary Whetton was going to start in the last test at Eden Park for the World XV.

The year 1992 would see the hundredth anniversary of the NZRU. The All Blacks were to play a three-test series against a World XV, marketed with the outrageously overstated title of the 'Clash of the Century'. In reality, it was a convenient way for the new-look All Blacks side to pick up a few morale-boosting wins after their World Cup disappointment. Except things didn't go according to script in the first game, when the World XV won

28–14 in Christchurch. Someone from the NZRU obviously went and reminded them of whose birthday it was, because the next test was a 54–26 shoot-out in the All Blacks' favour.

The series was destined to be a gimmicky anomaly. But then it emerged that former captain Gary Whetton was going to start in the last test at Eden Park for the World XV. The press went into a frenzy about his motivations to prove new coach Laurie Mains wrong for dumping him from the team, but unlike Colin Meads' Presidents XV upset in 1973, the game itself was nothing special. It ended as a regulation 26–15 win for the All Blacks, and Gary's performance was merely another day on the park. However, it did provide an apt career bookend for the now former All Blacks captain: his teammate that day was none other than Naas Botha, the Springbok legend he opposed in his first test on the same ground.

Now it was over. Gary Whetton had played 58 tests (a new All Blacks record, eclipsing the one held by Colin Meads), and 101 games in total for the All Blacks. AJ Whetton had 35 tests and 65 games in total, and went on to play in Japan.

Their careers didn't play out according to the script, but they were triumphant and fascinating all the same: Gary's career had started earlier than he would have thought, in a game that defies belief. AJ had to sit and watch from the bench for two years before he got his chance. Both decided to go on the Cavaliers tour, and both paid the price. They tasted World Cup glory alongside one another, and swept across the country in Auckland's long reign of success. Their faces, complete with trademark broad smiles, adorn the cover of the *1989 Rugby Almanack of New Zealand*, testament to their standing in that period of rugby history.

For the most part, they played for the same teams together.

While they didn't start together, their careers came to a close at the same time. They were casualties of a new broom being swept through the All Blacks as the country came to grips with the fact that they weren't the best team in the world any more.

The Whetton name lives on in New Zealand rugby. Gary's oldest son William plays professionally in France, while his younger son, Jack, is currently with the Highlanders. Gary is now an insurance consultant, while AJ is the general manager of a company that sells pitch-side advertising.

In today's highly structured world of pro rugby, the careers of William and Jack are probably not going to be anything like the way their father and uncle etched their names on All Blacks history. In a way, that's kind of a shame.

LEFT: Fred Woodman in the 1980s. Like his brother Kawhena, he is a North Auckland rugby stalwart. **PHOTOSPORT**

RIGHT: Kawhena Woodman in 1984. The brothers were brief All Blacks, but their legacy lives on in Kawhena's daughter Portia. **NEW ZEALAND RUGBY MUSEUM**

FRED AND KAWHENA WOODMAN

'ALL I HEARD GROWING UP WAS: Oh, is your dad Kawhena or Fred? Ohhhh, I played alongside your dad, he was a legend . . .'

She loves to talk about her whānau, it's obvious. Even though she says that Dad's time as a rugby player was a lifetime before she came along. Dad and Uncle Fred, that is. It's one thing to have a father who was an All Black, a Māori All Black and a North Auckland stalwart, but she has an uncle who was one, too.

These days she's the one who gets the headlines. Her name is Portia Woodman. The daughter of Kawhena Woodman, she's now the biggest name in women's rugby. There was every chance she could have played for the Silver Ferns, before she switched from netball to rugby in 2012. She has won a World Cup in both XVs and Sevens, and a Commonwealth Games gold medal. She once scored eight tries in a test match. But before she'd even picked up a ball, her dad and uncle had already woven the family's honour into the black jersey she'd end up starring in.

The Woodman brothers are from a different era to the one that Portia now dominates. There had been next to no serious games of women's rugby in the early '80s. Representative Sevens was still a bit of a muck-around drinking trip up to Hong Kong once a year. Women's Sevens didn't exist.

The province that we now know as Northland was called North Auckland, which is an odd name given that none of what is now the North Harbour union was actually in it. It was where Peter Jones had come down from in 1956 to score one of the most important tries ever and then tell the crowd he was absolutely buggered. Where Sid Going and his brothers and sons made sure their family name was on a team sheet for the better part of three decades. Where Norm Berryman, Warren Johnston, David Holwell and other cult heroes hailed from.

The Woodman brothers didn't have what you might call the most high-profile or classic All Blacks careers. Fred would play three tests and Kawhena none. Their careers spanned the late '70s to the late '80s, mostly running out on Okara Park in Whangarei.

Fred was the older brother. He was a tall, lean and fast winger who debuted in the Cambridge blue jersey of North Auckland in 1978 as a 20-year-old. It was an eventful year; they took the Ranfurly Shield from Manawatu late in the season but then refused to put it on the line for their final two games against Southland and Otago. While that didn't win them any friends, it showed the national selectors that Fred had the goods to step up.

That was the first aspect of a career that is basically a pub-trivia sports-section goldmine. He made his All Blacks debut against Fiji at Eden Park in 1980. The Fijians weren't deemed test-worthy back then, so it falls into the grey area between test matches and tour games. The match has its own significance of being against another nation, on New Zealand soil, but not officially an international. Fred had a good day out, scoring a try in the 33–0 win. Almost the same scenario occurred for his next game. The All Blacks stopped over in San Diego for a match against the United States later that season, on their way to the Welsh Rugby Union's centenary test match. Again Fred started on the wing, and picked up a try but not a test cap. It wasn't a great time to be a winger trying to bust your way into the All Blacks test XV, though. Wellington's Stu Wilson and Bernie Fraser had the two spots locked down tight and were in the prime of their careers, so it seemed like the only way Fred would make it was if one of those two got injured.

Fate has a funny way of working sometimes, though, because the next year was 1981, the infamous Springbok tour. Fred finally did get his break, but not because of being an injury replacement. Bruce Robertson withdrew from the team because of his objections to the tour, which meant that Wilson was moved to centre, and Fred came onto the wing for the first test at Lancaster Park.

> **Fate has a funny way of working sometimes, because the next year was 1981, the infamous Springbok tour. Fred finally did get his break, but not because of being an injury replacement.**

It's fair to say it wasn't a game for wingers. The All Blacks took the same sort of approach that the police and protesters had been adopting outside the grounds where the tour matches were being played, straight up in the faces of the Springboks in an exceptionally brutal, direct manner. While they did score three tries to none, the 14–9 win was a slugfest.

The next test in Wellington also saw the same backline combination retained. This game did see one of the wingers score, but unfortunately for Fred it was Gerrie Germishuys, the Springbok he was marking. It was the only try in a comprehensive 24–12 win to the Springboks. Fred was dropped for the decider, and got to watch what became known as the 'flour-bomb test' from the bench.

The All Blacks weren't finished with him yet, though. Fred ended up on the end-of-year tour, adding another test to his tally in Paris against France. He was done with All Blacks rugby after that, being able to boast that he'd scored tries in games against Fiji, the USA and a Romanian selection.

Not that he ever would boast about it. According to Portia, Uncle Fred is the quietest member of the Woodman family, preferring to let his deeds speak for themselves. His brother Kawhena, though—that's a different story.

Portia grew up in a household that was full of stories and recollections of her father's career. All sorts of different stories, from exploits for the teams he played for, to being allowed into a kitchen on a tour to Italy so he could provide the NZ Māori team with a boil-up. He was a stalwart in the North Auckland team, playing on the opposite wing to his brother.

According to Portia, Uncle Fred is the quietest member of the Woodman family, preferring to let his deeds speak for themselves. His brother Kawhena, though— that's a different story.

Kawhena's call-up to the All Blacks came somewhat out of the blue in the 1984 tour to Australia. Like his brother, he came in as a replacement for one of the team's stars. John Kirwan had been injured and Kawhena slotted into the midweek side for three games against New South Wales Country, Queensland Country and New South Wales B, scoring tries in the second and third games.

His All Blacks career came to an end the same way it started for Fred—against Fiji. The team toured the islands at the end of the 1984 season, again not giving the match against Fiji test status. Kawhena played in the three lead-up games, and scored his third and final try for the All Blacks on a stinking-hot day in Nadi on a field that would have been as hard as a carpark.

Ironically, the following year saw him get his only All Blacks trial. By now Kirwan and Craig Green had the test wing spots sewn up through to the World Cup and, like Fred, his international career was over.

You can see the pride in the Woodman brothers' eyes in their team photos. They're good-looking men in their early twenties, sporting two of the best moustaches that have ever been seen in the All Blacks. There is no doubt at all that Portia is Kawhena's daughter, both in her eyes and the way she plays.

She may have surpassed her dad and her Uncle Fred in terms of on-field deeds, but the way she talks about her dad speaks volumes of the regard she holds him in.

'He's been there and he's done that. Everything he did was for the love of the game; whatever input he can give me, I take it on board. In my eyes, he's my hero, my idol no matter what.'

Robin Brooke protects the ball for the Blues in the 1996 Super Rugby final, with Zinzan at his shoulder. The Brooke brothers were monumental contributors to Auckland, Blues and All Blacks rugby. **PHOTOSPORT**

ZINZAN AND ROBIN BROOKE

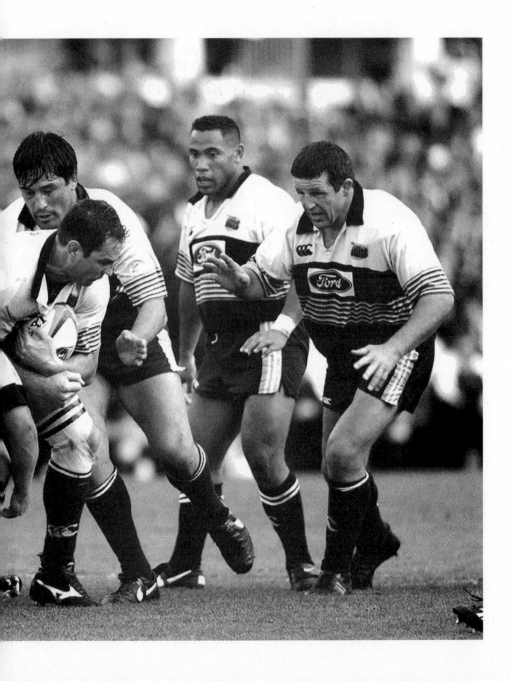

OPPORTUNITIES COME AND GO, in life and on a rugby field. What do you do when you're put on the spot? When you have to make a choice to play it safe or try something risky?

Like standing on halfway in a World Cup semi-final against England in Cape Town, 1995. The biggest game of your career so far. You've just punted down the touchline to pick out Rob Andrew, the English first five who is rattled so badly he's just hooked a penalty-goal attempt so wide it almost went over the touchline. Actually, all the Poms are rattled. Shell-shocked, even. Jonah Lomu opened the scoring by stomping a hole through their fullback Mike Catt on his way to the tryline. Then the rest of the backs followed that up by shredding the English for an 80-metre try. This game was supposed to be tight, these clowns beat us the last time we played them two years ago.

Andrew panics and sends a punt straight down your throat. The intent behind it is to just get the ball as far away as he possibly can, like he's sticking his head in the sand and trying to ignore that the score is 15–0 to the All Blacks after only a quarter of an hour. There's no one around you except your teammates. Weigh up your choices:

Run it straight back into the scattered English defence. They're all over the place; none of them want a bar of tackling right now.

Pass the ball. Try and get it out to Jonah again. If he gets a bit of space he'll be good for another try at least.

Or, if you're Zinzan Brooke, you take a third option. The goalposts are 50 metres away, and it's a beautiful day. So, despite being a number 8 with a considerable size advantage over most of your opposition, you line up a dropped goal. And you strike it perfectly. The crowd lets out a gasp of confusion, then a roar of approval. They're watching something only you would have the audacity to do. It flies end over end, straight over the black dot, 18–0. While the game isn't anywhere near half-time, it's as good as over. If Jonah's try was the knockout blow, this was the victory dance over the top of the comatose English. Maybe this will be the moment you'll be remembered for.

You strike it perfectly. The crowd lets out a gasp of confusion, then a roar of approval. They're watching something only you would have the audacity to do.

That's the way Zinzan Brooke played, and it seemed like all he ever did was make the right choice for the rest of the All Blacks to benefit. One of those All Blacks was his brother Robin, but this is a different tale than Colin Meads' epic career overshadowing that of Stan. This is one that bridges the divide between amateur and professional rugby, one that takes in one of All Blacks rugby's bitter disappointments and its greatest triumph. One that ushered in Super Rugby, and saw a number of controversies. The Brooke brothers were part of it all.

It may well have been Murray and Robin Brooke. Born 'Murray Zinzan', the older of the two later changed his name to

Zinzan Valentine, the new middle name coming on account of his birthday being 14 February. They were in the middle of a six-sibling set, brothers Naera, Marty and Simon, and sister Margaret. They grew up on a farm in Puhoi, north of Auckland, around animals and in an environment that Zinzan called 'the foundation of my life'.

> The freedom, the confidence Mum and Dad had in us kids and the way they pulled us all in so that even if we were deprived we were never made to feel it . . . Summers were not summers as so many city kids would understand them. No holidays away with the family . . . we spent our holidays cutting scrub or gorse or doing whatever needed to be done around the farm. Every day was another day's work, but we missed nothing.

Rugby, unsurprisingly, played a huge role in the boys' lives. They went to Mahurangi College, although Zinzan took the Colin Meads approach to secondary education and left aged 15. He and Robin grew up big, fast, and with the sort of on-field confidence that their childhood had instilled in them.

They moved south to the big city. Zinzan was there to study plumbing at polytech but that line of work took a back seat to rugby pretty quickly. He joined the Marist club, alongside a young winger called John Kirwan. His talent landed him a spot in the Auckland Under-18s, then the North Island Under-18s alongside a young flanker called Michael Jones. By the time he'd matured into playing seniors, he was a loose forward after spending time as a prop and lock.

Robin followed him and made the Auckland side in 1989,

when he came on to replace Gary Whetton. By the next season, he was the established other lock in the side, replacing his brother Marty.

Zinzan made the All Blacks first, as an openside flanker in the wider 1987 World Cup squad. He played one test in the tournament against Argentina and scored a try, running off a pass from Kirwan. The All Blacks loose forwards in the late '80s were as locked down as they'd ever be, though. Zinzan would have to wait behind Buck Shelford, AJ Whetton and Michael Jones for a first-choice spot for the time being, and Mark Brooke-Cowden was seen as a better choice to replace Jones when he was unavailable.

For the next couple of seasons Zinzan toured with the all-powerful All Blacks side that went unbeaten for 50 games. As well as that, he was a major part of the stunning success that John Hart's Auckland side was enjoying at the same time. Hart was to be the coach that would have the most influence over both brothers' careers, but for now Zinzan's All Blacks career was under the guidance of Grizz Wyllie.

In an ironic twist, it was the tough Cantabrian Wyllie that was to give the flashy Auckland loose forward his big break in 1990. As detailed in the Whetton brothers' story, Shelford was axed as captain and Brooke promoted to starting number 8.

'I don't think it was the declining of Buck Shelford. I just think it was the arriving of Zinzan Brooke,' said John Kirwan, who was privy to both the internal and external pressures the team was under.

It was also around this time that Zinzan fielded an opportunity that could have changed everything. He'd already expressed an interest in playing league earlier in his career, even contacting Wigan's Graham Lowe to gauge his interest. When 1990 rolled around, the now-Manly Sea Eagles coach Lowe was very interested in who he could acquire from the All Blacks, and made offers to both Zinzan and young fullback Matthew Ridge.

Zinzan and Ridge both signed their contracts, but the former reneged and stayed with union. In what must have been a particularly awkward moment, he hadn't told Ridge of his decision when they were both supposed to announce the news to their Auckland teammates. Ridge had already been upset that he wasn't getting as much money as Zinzan, then got left hanging as his supposed future league buddy sat tight-lipped in the team meeting.

It was to be Gary Whetton's eventual decline as the first-choice All Blacks lock that would ultimately open the door for Robin. The year 1992 saw a clean-out of the team, with Whetton gone as captain and a raft of new players picked under new coach Laurie Mains. Robin made his test debut that year in the home series against Ireland. However, while the Otago man and former All Blacks fullback clearly rated Robin, the same couldn't be said of his brother. Zinzan found himself on the outer with Mains, replaced by Arran Pene for that series and the first Bledisloe Cup test. The second was the first time he and Robin started a test together, and both also started the historic first post-apartheid test against the Springboks at Ellis Park that year.

It was in that game that Zinzan's impetuous ability to make something out of nothing first took centre stage. The All Blacks received a penalty close to the Springbok line, and, seeing that the opposition were clearly anticipating a shot at goal, he instinctively got hold of the ball and took a quick tap. He was untouched as he dived past a bunch of defenders all looking in the other direction for the game's first try.

Despite that moment of brilliance, Zinzan and Pene were to be interchanged frequently over the next couple of seasons. Robin's All Blacks career took its first speed bump too, as he found himself injured at the back end of the 1993 season. Mains was such a believer in Robin that he brought him on the end-of-season tour to England and Scotland in the hope that he'd get fit, only to see him earn the nickname 'Foodbill' and not play any matches.

That year, it was clear that the sunset of amateurism was upon the sport of rugby.

It took until the series win over the Springboks in 1994 that Zinzan finally nailed down Mains' approval, probably due to the utterly primitive way it was played. Again he was the nemesis of the Boks in the second test win in Wellington, marshalling his forward pack to score a slightly dodgy pushover try in which replays suggested the ball had clearly left the back of the scrum before Zinzan quickly hooked it back in with his left leg. He did have one cheeky long-range dropped-goal attempt that went wide of the posts just before half-time, though.

That year, it was clear that the sunset of amateurism was upon the sport of rugby. Zinzan's offer from Manly may have been refused, but it didn't stop plenty of others heading offshore and taking up league. In 1994, the latest first-choice All Black, John Timu, parted ways and made the march towards players having contracted jobs inevitable. But the old days weren't going to go quietly. One of the last displays of what the game used to be happened at Onewa Domain in the NPC final in 1994, and both Zinzan and Robin made headlines for all the wrong reasons.

The burning embers that burst into a violent firestorm that day were lit nine years previously when North Harbour broke away from Auckland to form their own union. Since then, North Harbour had been the classic little brother in a sibling rivalry. By the early '90s, though, they'd amassed enough talent to make them a serious force in the NPC. By '94, they were hosting Auckland in the final.

Their home ground at the time was a tiny park in Takapuna. It was barely more than a decent-sized club ground, and the decision to play it there made no sense. Because of the sides' previous fixture at Eden Park, it was decreed that the final be at North Harbour—despite the fact that they had finished below Auckland on the ladder. That's partly why it became known as the 'Battle of Onewa Domain'. The other reasons why were because the Auckland side, led by the Brookes, decided that they'd had enough of Harbour's upstart attitude and wanted to put them in their place once and for all.

It took a matter of minutes for the game to degenerate into the most ill-disciplined in NPC history.

The crowd had swollen to around 14,000 by the time the game kicked off. Onewa Domain was never designed to hold that many people, with a row of about a dozen portaloos along one of the touchlines obscuring the view for plenty of fans. If they'd maybe hopped up on the foul-smelling plastic boxes they would have seen something just as dirty happening out on the field, because it took a matter of minutes for the game to degenerate into the most ill-disciplined in NPC history.

Auckland started throwing punches, then Harbour started throwing them back. Robin got stuck in early. He clashed with Liam Barry, then went after Blair Larsen—both All Blacks teammates. Harbour winger Eric Rush decided to take matters into his own hands to put some heat back on the Aucklanders, and targeted a prone Zinzan while he watched a bomb sail over his head. Rush flew in like a missile while the ball was taken 10 metres upfield, cocking his elbow and connecting with the back of Zinzan's head, knocking him out cold.

What made it even more shocking is that Rush was, and indeed still is, considered to be one of the nice guys of rugby. Nevertheless, referee Colin Hawke had probably the easiest call of his career in ordering Rush off.

That wasn't the end of it, not by a long shot. Not long after, Robin's gripe with Larsen erupted into him stomping on the Harbour lock's head. Again, Hawke had no problem telling him to get off the park, and the game was reduced to 14 men each side after only 20 minutes. The rest of the game, won 22–16 by Auckland, was a spiteful affair to the final whistle. Seven players ended up being cited, and instead of being summoned to the NZRU judiciary, the judiciary was summoned to them, presumably to save a bit of money on air fares. The hearings took place at a motel near Auckland airport. Robin was suspended and the game has gone down in history as a classic example of what rugby was trying to move away from when it turned professional and started marketing itself properly.

Another relic of the past was to be the next big turning point in Zinzan's career. The year 1995 was a big one: the All Blacks were going into a seriously competitive World Cup and Mains had only one test beforehand to warm the team up. It's fair to say his squad was more or less locked in before the season started, but there was a trial match held in Hamilton regardless. Unfortunately for Zinzan, it ended with him seriously damaging his Achilles tendon.

The race was on to get himself ready in time for the tournament, which was only five weeks away. The rehabilitation sessions in a decompression chamber were arduous. So arduous, they eventually ended up being the basis of a Steinlager ad in which Zinzan admitted that his desperation to be healed meant that if someone had told him that putting fried eggs on his leg would help, he probably would have believed them.

Meanwhile, Robin had been injured as well in the All Blacks' first test of the year against Canada. The brothers were now passengers on the squad that headed to South Africa to try to win back the World Cup, and Laurie Mains wasn't going to take any chances with either of them. The team's first match against Ireland was only the second time in three seasons that neither Brooke was included in the starting XV. They missed the next game against Wales, but were both set to make their comebacks against Japan.

This was probably the worst game in history to get a gauge on how well a rugby player has recovered from an injury. The All Blacks side made up of their wider squad members massacred the Japanese 145–17, and Mains probably would have got a better read on Zinzan and Robin's fitness if he'd sent them for a run up a hill. It was a memorable match for Robin, though, who outplayed his brother by scoring two tries to none.

Turns out it was enough for them both to be reinstated into the top side for the quarter-final against Scotland, though. In any other time, two key players coming back into the test side for such a crucial match would have been a big deal. However, everything was being literally overshadowed by the giant figure of Jonah Lomu and the effect he was having on the tournament and the entire sport.

The Scots found that out, but it wasn't like they were ever going to beat the All Blacks in their quarter-final. The showdown with England in Cape Town was to become arguably the quintessential All Blacks World Cup performance, albeit in a tournament they didn't end up winning. The final score was 45–29, most remembered for Lomu's four tries and Zinzan's outrageous dropped goal. It's worth mentioning too that by now both brothers had completely played their way back into fitness and Laurie Mains' favour. Despite the scoreline, this was a real test against a team that genuinely went in feeling as though they could replicate their 1993 victory, and got their World Cup dreams utterly destroyed instead. It was about now that the familiar combination of R. M. Brooke and I. D. Jones started being two names that you could be assured would be next to one another for the time being.

Everything was being literally overshadowed by the giant figure of Jonah Lomu and the effect he was having on the tournament and the entire sport.

Then came the final. Rainbow Nation, food poisoning, a 747 flying over Ellis Park. Zinzan and Robin shook hands with a Bok-jersey-wearing Nelson Mandela, probably something neither of them ever thought they'd do when they first started playing for the All Blacks. This time, though, it was to be another dropped goal that the game would be remembered for. Unfortunately for the All Blacks, it was by Joel Stransky to win the game 15–12 in extra time. The world watched as Francois Pienaar hoisted the trophy alongside Mandela. Hollywood made a movie about it and forgot to cast someone as Suzie the waitress.

But it wasn't going to be long until the All Blacks could get their revenge. While the early '90s were a tumultuous period for the team, the next couple of years would see them going back to being unquestionably the best team in the world—if not the actual official one.

Before then, though, there was to be a prominent role for the Brooke brothers in the first-ever official professional game of rugby played in New Zealand. Zinzan led the Auckland Blues out on the Palmerston North Showgrounds for a win over the Wellington Hurricanes, signalling the new era of top-tier rugby in New Zealand. Both he and Robin would play prominent roles in the Blues' inaugural campaign, which ended in them thumping the Natal Sharks 45–21 in the final at Eden Park. Zinzan became the first man to lift the Super 12 trophy and, given that the Blues side was stacked with test players, the result was an ominous warning to the other test-playing nations that the World Cup final failure wasn't going to have any lasting effects on the All Blacks' will to win.

The All Blacks would make up for the World Cup heartbreak in 1996. In a way, it's fair to say that the tour to South Africa probably was the more daunting prospect for the team. It was their last chance to achieve a test series win on South African soil and most people knew that full well, despite professional rugby being in place for only a year. The tour had been brokered before the switch, but had the new Tri Nations series attached to the front of it. This was the way rugby was going to be from now on, but the first-ever edition of the tournament had a decidedly old-school look about it when it started.

The brothers' Auckland coach John Hart was now calling the shots for the All Blacks. It seemed a natural fit in the professional era, with Hart being the fast-talking, managerial type that was the next stage along from gruff former test players Mains and Wyllie who had preceded him. Hart would stay in charge of the side for the rest of Zinzan and Robin's careers.

The opening match took place at the by-now crumbling Athletic Park in Wellington. Just like it had been time and time again in the capital for a rugby test, it was an absolutely atrocious day after an atrocious week of weather. The All Blacks had trained midweek at Wellington College, and had chosen to do their scrum practice on the cricket-pitch block while the first XI coach and groundskeeper watched on in horror. Everything was set up for this to be a tough, kick-based encounter and the Wallabies had fond memories of their last visit there in 1990. It was a similar day then, too, back when Zinzan was still at the centre of controversy surrounding his replacement of Buck Shelford.

The rain and wind howled through the park as the crowd shivered in their Swanndris and Driza-Bones. A cannon went off as the teams set foot on the field; underneath the Millard Stand the shock of the blast dislodged decades' worth of rust and sent it showering down on the crowd that had thought themselves fortunate to have got out of the rain. However, the effects of that were as nothing compared to what was about to happen to the Wallabies. Especially after they chose to huddle on their own 22 during the haka, drawing the ire of the entire country.

They call it the greatest All Blacks performance of all time. 'They' being the ones who were there to see it and experience the conditions that the team had to overcome, and the ones who watched on TV and were just as stunned. It's probably fair to lump the Wallabies in with that group as well; they had a better view than anyone of just how well the All Blacks played on 6 July 1996.

It took only two minutes for the All Blacks to grab the lead. Despite the wind and rain, Robin claimed a perfect ball in the middle of the lineout and set up a drive for Michael Jones to score. It was the first-ever try that would pay out as a winner at the TAB, which is more than a little ironic given Jones' devoutly religious views that prevented him from playing on Sundays, let alone entertain a vice like gambling. Like so many times before in All Blacks test matches, the die was already cast. There was to be 78 more minutes of misery for the Wallabies, and now it was Zinzan's turn to be a provider.

He chimed into the backline soon after and floated a perfect pass to Christian Cullen to stroll over. After Justin Marshall galloped 40 metres into the teeth of the southerly to score in one corner, Zinzan came off the back of the scrum and dived in to score in the other. Half-time read 25–6, and now the All Blacks had the wind in the second half.

By now, the rain had turned the normally lush field into a churned-up mess. By the time Zinzan rampaged down the wing to set up Jeff Wilson's try, it was almost impossible to tell the teams apart for all the mud that was now covering their uniforms. Well, impossible apart from the fact that the Wallabies were the ones spending time hanging out behind their own goal line looking like they regretted ever deciding to play rugby when they were kids. The final damage: 43–6. It's one of the definitive scorelines of All Blacks history.

A fortnight later, though, it was a different story. The world champion Springboks rolled into Christchurch and gave the All Blacks the old-school battle that typified the two teams' rugby relationship with one another. You'd be doing well to find highlights of this match anywhere—the All Blacks won 15–11 and again failed to score a try. It was, though, the first of five matches they would play against each other that year. Zinzan and Robin would start and finish every single one.

After a nail-biting win over a vastly improved Wallabies team the next week in Brisbane (notable for an outrageous flurry of punches by Michael Brial on Frank Bunce in retribution for a bit of foul play the All Blacks midfielder had dished out during the 1992 tour of Australia), the touring squad assembled for their ultimate challenge—what would be the last-ever full All Blacks tour to South Africa.

Zinzan remembered in one of his columns for *The Telegraph* just what sort of brutality awaited them:

> It won't happen now with all the concussion protocols, but when you got half knocked out in my day you stayed on the pitch against them. Don't show pain. Don't show weakness. Of all the teams you faced, you never wanted to show them you were hurt because they thrived off that.

Everything the All Blacks had strived for in the past when they went to South Africa—rightly or wrongly—was about to play out over the next four weeks. In a sign of the changing times it wasn't a four-test series—the first one in Cape Town was the last match in the Tri Nations, which counted for nothing as far as the tournament was concerned because the All Blacks had already won. However, it was a chance to finally break the All Blacks' try-scoring duck against the Boks, which stretched all the way back to Zinzan's pushover at Athletic Park in 1994. The game was won 29–18, but it took until deep into the second half for Glen Osborne to finally cross for a try. It had been 390 minutes between five-pointers against the Springboks.

At the end of the match Sean Fitzpatrick was presented with the comically oversized Tri Nations trophy. Again, in another sign that amateurism hadn't quite been done away with just yet, whoever made the trophy had mistaken the dimensions somehow and it was almost big enough for Fitzpatrick to bathe in. In a style befitting his reputation as a man who would never shirk from a decent product placement, the All Blacks skipper made sure he had a bottle of Powerade in one hand despite the awesome effort it took to hoist the massive piece of silverware over his head.

At the end of the match Sean Fitzpatrick was presented with the comically oversized Tri Nations trophy . . . whoever made it had mistaken the dimensions somehow and it was almost big enough for Fitzpatrick to bathe in.

It would probably be the least celebrated trophy win the All Blacks ever had. That was just the start of their South African campaign, and it carried on the next week in Durban with the first official test of the series. The Springboks heightened tensions by picking Henry Tromp at hooker, who had been convicted of killing a black labourer on his farm three years previously, erasing a significant amount of goodwill that their World Cup win had garnered. Again, it was a tight battle, but it was becoming obvious that the speed and skill of the All Blacks backs was providing the biggest problem for the Springboks. While they'd won the World Cup and made a successful re-entry into the test arena, it was obvious that they didn't have anywhere near the same ability out wide that the current crop of All Blacks possessed.

The Durban test did produce three All Blacks tries in the corners of the Kings Park field, one each to Jeff Wilson and Christian Cullen. That second try was due to a bit of Zinzan brilliance, flicking a sweet pass wide to the fullback before getting levelled in a tackle by the defender he'd just drawn in to give Cullen a free run to the line. The last crucial score he made himself after lurking out wide. Wilson had latched onto a hopeful cross-field kick by Walter Little, and the ball eventually made it to Zinzan's hands for an epic 20-metre run to dive over and seal the game.

All of a sudden, all the World Cup pressure was back on as the team prepared for the next test in Pretoria. If the result in Wellington earlier in the season had become a symbol for just how good the All Blacks were despite awful weather conditions, the second test in Pretoria showed just how much the team would do to achieve the one thing that would mean the absolute most.

What unfolded on the afternoon of 24 August 1996 at Loftus Versfeld (early Sunday morning New Zealand time) ended up being the greatest day in All Blacks history. Loose-fitting cotton jerseys, slightly grainy footage, a field that looked as barren as an Indian cricket pitch.

It started with a violent statement of intent by the Springboks. They weren't there to simply roll over and die, and they scored the first try after Hannes Strydom bashed his way over after only three minutes.

The All Blacks struck back almost straight away. Robin picked up a pass from Justin Marshall after the halfback had made a break on halfway. His next move was to fling a perfectly timed but ever-so-slightly forward pass to Ian Jones, who gave it to Wilson to trot in under the posts. Wilson followed it up with a brilliant solo effort, but now it was Zinzan's turn. Off a five-metre scrum the All Blacks ran a beautifully executed play that saw him one-on-one with Stransky. A first five on a number 8 is never going to be a fair fight, and Stransky, the hero from the year before, was swatted off like an irritating bug: 21–11 at half-time. This was suddenly looking all too easy for the All Blacks.

Of course, this probably wouldn't be a tale worthy of such epic status if the Boks didn't mount an impressive comeback. It came in the form of two second-half tries to Ruben Kruger and Joost van der Westhuizen. The latter made up for the forward pass that Robin had thrown to set up the All Blacks' first try, as the mad scramble that saw the Bok halfback score definitely included at least one knock-on. The score now sat at 24–23.

Time for some heroics.

Jon Preston had just come onto the field, and his first act was a 40-metre penalty goal. His second was from 52 metres, confidently calling for the kicking tee despite Fitzpatrick suggesting that Wilson take it. Stransky goaled one in between and the All Blacks bench was being called upon as the starting players began to succumb to the intensity of the match: 30–26.

By now the All Blacks were out on their feet anyway, needing to hang in for the final bell to end the fight. Once again, base skill level was going to prove the difference, with the Boks just not having the firepower out wide to be able to run the length of the field to snatch back the lead.

An All Blacks try would have put it out of doubt, but after the World Cup final it would be more fitting to deliver the fatal blow with a dropped goal. There was only one man in the team who had kicked a successful droppie in test matches before, but even then no one expected Zinzan to produce an even more audacious strike than his one against England. After a good run by Frank Bunce, he dropped back into the pocket behind the ruck after noticing that the Bok forwards were spread out across the field. Too spread out to have a decent crack at a charge-down.

He barked at Marshall to give him the ball. The halfback popped up, swivelled around and instinctively passed, but the look on his face when he realised it was Zinzan somewhat belied the fact that this was not a planned move. With only one Bok defender pressuring him, Zinzan steadied and banged the ball through the uprights, leaning ever so slightly to his right as if he was willing a tee shot to land on the fairway: 33–26.

It wasn't over yet. The All Blacks still had a torrid goal-line stand to deal with as the Springboks desperately tried to protect their unbeaten home record. It ended, fittingly, a metre out from the line with the exhausted All Blacks forwards finally stifling one last charge. Robin ended the game with his hands on the ball in the last collapsed maul, while Zinzan stood behind him waiting for the next assault. The ref blew his whistle, and it was done—arms raised to the heavens, before Zinzan toppled backwards onto his own tryline, utterly spent from the pure exertion that the last 80 minutes had wrought. Barely a metre away, Fitzpatrick was on his knees, pounding the turf in recognition of what they'd just achieved.

The All Blacks captain led his team on a victory lap of Loftus, making sure he had his bottle of Powerade in full view. All of the efforts of the All Blacks over the last 68 years had been realised. Zinzan had given highlight compilers a shot for the ages with his celebration of the dropped goal, and he and Robin had ensured that their names would be on the list of the third, and last, All Blacks team to get their own title.

Barely a metre away, Fitzpatrick was on his knees, pounding the turf in recognition of what they'd just achieved.

Despite dropping the last test in Johannesburg, the 1996 team returned home to be dubbed 'The Incomparables'. So far, so good for the All Blacks in the new era of professional rugby. It was also around this time that Zinzan was making serious noises about quitting New Zealand rugby for another opportunity overseas— he was 31 by now but in hindsight it seemed a little hasty as he was in some of the best form of his life.

If the Blues were good in 1996, they were unstoppable in 1997. Again Zinzan was given the captaincy and led the side to an unbeaten season, with the only game they didn't win being a crazy 40-all draw against Northern Transvaal. The final was another one-sided affair, although rain at Eden Park meant that the Brumbies held the score to 23–7. In two seasons the Blues had scored 843 points and won 18 games. It looked as though the competition was simply going to be a continuation of Auckland's provincial dominance over the last decade; that Super Rugby was set for a dynasty of Blues title wins. Not everyone was enamoured with Auckland's success, though. Something was brewing down south and the first major blow to the dominance that Zinzan's team had enjoyed was to come at the end of the domestic season.

There was the matter of some test matches to get through first. The All Blacks simply picked up where they left off the year before and destroyed Fiji and Argentina in their early matches. The first test against the Pumas was especially fun for Zinzan and Robin, with the game turning into a 93–8 turkey shoot and giving them a chance to really showcase their open-field skills. Deep in the second half, Zinzan took a pass after a break-out from the All Blacks 22, then instinctively kicked across the field for Robin to beat Fitzpatrick to the ball as it rolled perfectly over the tryline. Not long after, Fitzpatrick told the referee to call the game off eight minutes early so the Argentines wouldn't have the ignominy of conceding 100 points.

Something was brewing down south and the first major blow to the dominance that Zinzan's team had enjoyed was to come at the end of the domestic season.

Again, though, the highlight of the season was against the Springboks, and this time the All Blacks banished another ghost of the World Cup final loss. The pulsating 35–32 win came at Ellis Park, a venue at which the All Blacks hadn't beaten the Springboks since 1928.

With the Tri Nations locked up, the All Blacks returned to NPC duty. This was to be Zinzan's last campaign for Auckland; by now he'd led them to four titles in a row, but it wasn't going to have the sort of send-off that he would have liked. The season ended up conspiring to have them play a semi-final at Lancaster

Park in front of a typically hostile Canterbury crowd. In a sign of the shift of power that was about to happen in New Zealand rugby, the home side strangled the life out of Auckland's much-vaunted attack and relied on Andrew Mehrtens' boot to get them to an 18–15 lead late in the match.

It was time for Zinzan to either take it like the stoic sort of rugby player that New Zealand is known for, or go all in and let rip with about 20 years' worth of pent-up frustration against referees.

Zinzan had been clearly aggrieved with the way Paddy O'Brien was refereeing the game. Canterbury pressed hard on the Auckland line, so when they won possession off a reasonably straightforward turnover call, it was time for Zinzan to either take it like the stoic sort of rugby player that New Zealand is known for, or go all in and let rip with about 20 years' worth of pent-up frustration against referees.

He chose the latter. After angrily shoving away teammate Charles Riechelmann, who attempted to restrain him, Zinzan got about as close as he could to O'Brien and demanded an explanation. The whistleblower told him to go away, so Zinzan did—back to his line to yell at O'Brien that the call was a 'f**king joke'. He then doubled down after the game had been lost 21–15, giving an interview that didn't exactly suggest he was sorry at all for what he'd said. It wasn't the classiest end to his illustrious provincial career, because the loss meant it was the last time he'd pull on an Auckland jersey.

But he wasn't done yet. The All Blacks' supreme form meant that the end-of-year tour to England was seen as a mere formality, with two tests against them and one against Wales in between.

The All Blacks' test against Wales was a regulation hiding. That's no surprise given how low Welsh rugby was at the time— they'd been knocked out of the pool stages of the World Cup two years before, finished bottom of the Five Nations and were not far away from almost getting 100 points put on them by the Springboks. The most notable thing about the match was that it was at Wembley, used by the Welsh as a home ground while the new Millennium Stadium was being constructed in Cardiff. Robin showed his skill by setting up Christian Cullen for two of his three tries that day, while Zinzan displayed trademark cheekiness to flick the ball through his legs from the back of a scrum to send Marshall over. But there was time for one last piece of Zinzan Brooke magic for the highlight reels.

Of the three dropped goals that Zinzan landed in his test career, this was definitely the most meaningless, and the most obviously self-indulgent. Once again, he lined up behind Marshall from 30 metres out and slammed home the kick to make the score 42–7. Those would be the last points he'd score in an All Blacks jersey. If his career were a movie, that's when the credits should have rolled.

Except it wasn't, and his last game was a 26-all draw the next weekend against England. The All Blacks treated it like a loss and it probably should have been one after the English raced out to a 20–3 lead after 20 minutes. Zinzan's association with New Zealand rugby ended in London, which was fitting because that's where his life would be based from then on.

He signed to play for the famous Harlequins club, and ended up being coached by his former All Blacks teammate John Gallagher.

Eventually, he took over Gallagher's role as a player/coach. Things went all right for the first year at Quins, but they plummeted to the bottom of the English Premiership by the end of 2000. Only a week out from a semi-final in the midweek Anglo-Welsh Cup at the start of 2001, Zinzan resigned.

This wasn't the end of it for the Brooke brothers, though. In fact, for Robin, he was about to enter perhaps the greatest period of angst the All Blacks had ever suffered. If 1996 and '97 were the golden years, '98 and '99 were to be ones that All Blacks fans will want to forget. His brother now gone and playing out his career in England, Robin would battle on in a team that was severely shorn of talent and experience.

It was such a stunning fall from grace that most fans of that era will often turn their heads away in disgust when that year is mentioned.

On reflection, 1998 was probably the worst All Blacks season of all time. Yes, the 1949 team lost one more test, but four of them were in South Africa against dodgy referees and without some of their best players. They were also coming off two years' worth of inactivity. The '98 side, however, was continuing from perhaps the best period in All Blacks history and had the advantage of the game now being professional. It was such a stunning fall from grace that most fans of that era will often turn their heads away in disgust when that year is mentioned.

Five losses. In a row. Never mind that two of them were incredibly close and came down to the last few minutes, and the second loss to the Springboks was due to a try that should never have been given. While Robin battled on in the second row, the cast around him had a very different look to the one that had dominated for the last couple of seasons. Sean Fitzpatrick's spot was now taken by Anton Oliver. Zinzan's was filled by Taine Randell, Isitolo Maka and Xavier Rush throughout the year. Olo Brown and Craig Dowd were swapped out for Carl Hoeft and Kees Meeuws. Even the ever-present Ian Jones was replaced by Royce Willis. This disruption to the forwards did the most damage to the All Blacks' fortunes, and the absence of Fitzpatrick's leadership left a giant hole that the young Randell couldn't fill.

The public didn't need much of an excuse to completely turn on Hart, whose Auckland ways had been rubbing the rest of New Zealand the wrong way despite his outstanding run of results up until that point.

Forward planning hadn't come into fruition. Game plans were tossed out after one attempt. The public didn't need much of an excuse to completely turn on Hart, whose Auckland ways had been rubbing the rest of New Zealand the wrong way despite his outstanding run of results up until that point.

This may well have been the time for Robin to step up and become captain himself. By now, he was the most experienced player on the team, and it would have been a logical move given that he was still an automatic selection. But things weren't going so smoothly at the Blues and it was this situation that did the most damage to his captaincy aspirations. The Blues made the

Super 12 final again in 1998, but the core of the Canterbury side that had shown Zinzan's provincial career the door had re-formed as the Crusaders side that eventually beat the Blues in a thrilling final at Eden Park.

The following year was the first slide down a cascading trail of misery that's been part of the Blues experience ever since. Coach Graham Henry left, with the NZRU somehow appointing Taranaki's Jed Rowlands to the job. They had a new captain, too, with Robin taking over from Michael Jones. The relationship between the new skipper and coach, or lack thereof, could be seen as a blight on Robin's career. While many thought that Rowlands was never up to the job, the lack of support he got from his senior players was palpable.

According to longtime broadcaster Murray Deaker, writing in the *New Zealand Herald* on 30 June 2000, Rowlands was

> shafted by Blues players too gutless to tell Rowlands to his face that they believed he couldn't coach but were prepared to meet behind closed doors to write a damning report after the season was lost . . . gutted by the media, lied to by his employers, snitched on by his players, Jed Rowlands has been the personification of the naive, honest, country lad cleaned out and tarnished forever by urbane, self-seeking rugby politicians anxious to save their own butts.

While that's a little bit overblown, it did represent what the wider rugby community felt about the situation. To make Robin captain of the All Blacks would have brought all that baggage with it, so Randell was retained despite already being the least successful leader in a season, ever.

It also didn't help that Hart was going into a World Cup year essentially having to start over in terms of preparation. Robin found himself with a new man to put his arm around in the scrums; Norm Maxwell seemed to be a like-for-like replacement for the now retired Ian Jones, a tall, safe lineout option that even came from Northland as well. They started every test in the lead-up to the World Cup together, and it seemed like the All Blacks were getting back on track after the shock of '98. Two wins over the Boks and one over the Wallabies at home were offset by a 28–7 loss to the Australians in Sydney. It remains the largest margin of victory anyone has ever achieved over the All Blacks, and tellingly showed that they still hadn't quite regained the dominance in the forwards that would be necessary to win a World Cup.

Because that's what the 1999 All Blacks season is remembered for. Not the whole World Cup, just one game. One opponent. One period of play. One horrific memory that sticks out for New Zealanders probably more than the entire previous season combined: France. Twickenham.

It was as if lightning had struck them over and over again and the residual burn effect scarred the entire country for another 12 years.

Like Gary Whetton, the man whose place he'd originally filled back in 1992, Robin's All Blacks career would come to an end in a shock World Cup semi-final loss. It was as if lightning had struck them over and over again and the residual burn effect scarred the entire country for another 12 years. For those too young to remember but also for people who have blocked it out of their memory, this was supposed to be a walk in the park for the All Blacks. France had fallen arse-first into the semi-final, almost losing to Fiji in the pool stages, and had been demolished 54–7 by the All Blacks back in June of that year. While everyone probably can recall the over-the-top marketing effort before the World Cup that saw the All Blacks front row painted on the side of an Air New Zealand jet, it is also worth remembering that by now, Jonah Lomu was back to his best form—some might argue better than 1995. He'd played a huge hand in beating England at Twickenham in their pool match and by half-time in the semi-final had already scored a try.

What happened next is usually described as 20 minutes that sunk the hopes of an entire nation and ultimately cost the All Blacks a World Cup final spot.

What happened next is usually described as 20 minutes that sunk the hopes of an entire nation and ultimately cost the All Blacks a World Cup final spot. But the reality is it was only around five minutes: Christophe Dominici's and then Richard Dourthe's tries, one straight after the other, is what killed the All Blacks; Philippe Bernat-Salles' try 10 minutes later was completely against the run of play. Despite having almost complete domination of territory and possession in the match, the All Blacks came up well short due to a French team that seemed to be getting dealt blackjack with every hand (if you're still gutted about this game, find the version with French commentary on YouTube, which is heartwarmingly hilarious).

Final score: 43–31. The Brooke brothers' era in the All Blacks was over, 13 years after Zinzan had first pulled on the jersey. Zinzan's final game was a forgettable draw, but Robin's was to become the biggest test-match post-mortem ever. John Hart resigned and Randell was replaced as captain. The public backlash bordered on insanity at times, with Hart's horse having beer thrown on it at a race meeting in Auckland.

New coach Wayne Smith didn't need 34-year-old Robin for the 2000 All Blacks. Instead, he picked Troy Flavell as his replacement, and it proved to be a good choice as Robin's Blues teammate scored a hat-trick on debut against Tonga. Flavell appeared to emulate both the good and bad aspects of Robin's career—showing remarkable skill at times during his eventual 22-test career, as well as getting himself a lengthy suspension for stomping on the head of Chiefs player Greg Smith during a Super 12 game in 2003, just like Robin had done back in 1994.

Zinzan is widely regarded as the greatest number 8 to have ever played the game, and his 17 test tries set a record for a forward until Richie McCaw surpassed it.

Robin ended up captaining the Blues for another two seasons before hanging up his boots at the end of 2001. He'd played 62 tests, second only to Ian Jones for an All Blacks lock and four more than his illustrious brother. He and Jones had formed a partnership of 49 tests together in the second row, a record that stood until 2018 when it was broken by Brodie Retallick and

Samuel Whitelock. Instead of joining Zinzan offshore, he bought into a supermarket franchise that is often held up as a model for professional players transitioning into a successful career post-rugby. Meanwhile, by 2015 Zinzan had established himself as CEO of a new construction business.

The legacy of the Brooke brothers is an indelible mark on All Blacks history. Zinzan is widely regarded as the greatest number 8 to have ever played the game, and his 17 test tries set a record for a forward until Richie McCaw surpassed it. Robin's career could have had far more test caps had he not been dogged with injury in the early years, and it's fair to say that out of all the brothers in this book, he is the one whose career stands alongside his sibling's.

They are the giants of the pre-modern era. Two brothers that carried a team through some of the greatest and also the most tragic of All Blacks moments.

STEPHEN AND GRAEME BACHOP

ONE IS FONDLY REMEMBERED AS one of the best halfbacks to ever wear the All Blacks jersey. The other was one of the best first fives to wear the blue of Samoa. Both played in what could be remembered as one of the All Blacks' finest test-series wins, but oddly isn't. Both went to four World Cups between them, but only one for the All Blacks. They spent most of their careers playing against one another.

The Bachops' story saw, between them, the wearing of Canterbury, Otago, All Blacks, Samoan, Hurricanes, Highlanders, Sanix, London Irish and Japanese colours. Oh, and a brief stint in the historical anomaly that was the Central Vikings.

It began in Christchurch. Stephen, the elder of the two, was born in 1966. Graeme followed a year later. The boys grew up playing as a combo; Graeme developed as a snappy passing halfback while Stephen ran outside him at first five. Neither was particularly big, and both went to Hagley High School where they played in the first XV together, then for the Linwood club. By 1987, they were both renowned enough to be picked for the NZ Colts.

Graeme got his call-up to the All Blacks at the end of that year, after the World Cup had been won and David Kirk's retirement. The team headed to Japan to play some commercially driven fixtures in a market that would eventually end up hosting its own

World Cup. Graeme was competing with another All Blacks brother for the starting test halfback spot in Bruce Deans. Both men were from Canterbury and would stay under the tutelage of Grizz Wyllie for both their provincial and international careers for the time being. Though the games in Japan weren't given test status, Deans gained the spot the next year. Graeme had to wait 13 games and another year and a half to finally get a test start against Wales when Deans was injured.

All of those 13 games were comfortable wins. His test debut was no different. The All Blacks thrashed the Welsh 34–9, in a game that was mostly notable for Richard Loe having a try disallowed despite slamming the ball over the line so hard he left a decent-sized divot in the Cardiff Arms Park turf. That was the turning point for Graeme, though; his display leapfrogged him ahead of Deans and into the number 9 jersey for the next two seasons.

That would include the 1991 World Cup. This is where Stephen and Graeme's careers would intersect, not quite colliding but definitely coming out the other end with very different memories.

By now, Stephen had shifted south to Otago, where he played for the Southern club. He was eligible to play for Western Samoa, so took the opportunity to play in their debut appearance at the tournament. While the '91 World Cup is remembered as a failure of grand proportions by the all-powerful All Blacks, the Samoan experience was very much the opposite. The scrappy underdogs that everyone grew to love pulled off a stunning 16–13 upset of Wales in their first game, then qualified for the quarter-finals with a win against Argentina and a narrow loss to the eventual champion Wallabies. While they were comprehensively defeated by a very strong Scotland side in their knockout match, they had won the respect of rugby fans around the world.

The World Cup hadn't been great for Graeme, though. Burdened with the expectation that the All Blacks would swamp their opposition and retain the Cup, only to be beaten handily by the Wallabies in their semi-final, he was part of the clean-out that was to happen under Laurie Mains' tenure as coach the following year. Stephen's performances for Samoa had clearly had the opposite effect on Mains, who also happened to be his coach at Otago. Thanks to the eligibility laws back then being essentially non-existent, and the attitude of New Zealand administrators towards Pacific Island rugby that hasn't really changed much to this day, he was allowed to swap the blue of Samoa for a black jersey in 1992.

Like his brother, though, Stephen would have to play out a number of tour games before he'd get a crack at a test spot. In fact, it was one more than Graeme's total, with 14 games spread out over tours to Australia, South Africa and the UK. One of them ended up being the All Blacks' heaviest defeat ever, a 40–17 loss to Sydney. The strange fixture was the only time a team representing the city and not the state of New South Wales was on the tour schedule; in any event it comprised plenty of current Wallabies and lined up against an All Blacks team severely lacking any sort of experience.

In the test matches, Grant Fox was still very much the first-choice first five until his retirement in 1993, and in his injury-enforced absence Mains used Walter Little, then Marc Ellis immediately after Fox had hung up the boots.

The Bachop brothers finally got to be together in a test match in 1994. It was an odd season for the All Blacks; Mains still hadn't finished his tinkering to rebuild the side before the World Cup the following year, and it showed in their mid-year series against France. He had again brought in a new first five, this time giving Simon Mannix a start ahead of Stephen. The test was a 22–8 loss, which remains France's largest-ever margin of victory over the All Blacks. Stephen finally got his first test start against them the following week. It would be a game that would go down in history—though not the way he would have hoped.

It ended with a try so famous it eventually got its own name. *L'essai du bout du monde*—the try from the end of the world. With a name like that, let alone the absolute perfection in which it was executed, it's pretty hard for All Blacks fans to be too upset at the French for pulling off a scoring movement that won the game and sealed a French series victory on New Zealand soil for the first time ever. All Stephen would have been concerned about while he was standing under the Eden Park goalposts after it had happened, though, was that it was his aimless kick down into the hands of French winger Philippe Saint-André that started it all.

It ended with a try so famous it eventually got its own name. *L'essai du bout du monde*—the try from the end of the world.

Seven passes and 80 metres later, and fullback Jean-Luc Sadourny scored the winner. Stephen pops up in the often-replayed fantastic voyage that the ball takes to the tryline, as one of the many All Blacks left clutching at thin air as the French players combined to inscribe their names in history. If you drew a line between him and his teammates in their shocking defensive effort on the try, it would have looked like a cardiac arrest on a heart-rate monitor—and that's a fair reflection of how the country was feeling about rugby in 1994. Things weren't about to get any easier, because while the All Blacks had been losing to France, the Springboks had landed in New Zealand for a full tour and three test matches.

The 1994 Springbok tour occupies a strange place in the memory banks of rugby fans in New Zealand. The series victories in 1956, '65 and (whichever way you want to remember it) '81 are talked about as massive moments in All Blacks history, and this was to be the first tour the Springboks engaged in after their readmission to international rugby. The two sides had played each other two years previously in Johannesburg in a one-off test, but these were still the days when matters had to be settled over a test series and a bunch of provincial games in between.

The first odd thing was that, compared to the intervals between past tours to New Zealand, the 13-year gap was actually about right when it came to having the Springboks over. In fact, it was shorter than the time that had passed between tours previously. Statistically, the apartheid ban had barely affected relations between the two teams at all—especially if you consider that the All Blacks effectively did play the Springboks in 1986 on the unofficial Cavaliers tour.

This was to be the series where the Bachop brothers finally got to line up alongside one another. Graeme, after two years of watching Ant Strachan, Stu Forster and Jon Preston takes turns in the halfback spot, was returned by Mains to the starting XV. Stephen retained his spot despite the loss to the French. Their first experience as a 9–10 combination came in the opening test at Carisbrook.

There were a couple of newcomers in the All Blacks that day, too. Alama Ieremia slotted in at second five outside Stephen, while Shane Howarth came in at fullback. Rugby loves its traditions, or at least makes out like it does, so Laurie Mains had instructed the side to play a win-at-all-costs brand of rugby that was the way the All Blacks and Springboks had gone about their matches for the previous 73 years. This wasn't so much a test, more the opening few rounds in a heavyweight title fight.

Despite the ground and conditions being perfect for a free-flowing game, the two sides quickly set their game plans to ultra-conservative and Stephen kicked more often than not. When he did let it go, his pass cannoned into the side of Ieremia's head. It was the second five's first touch of the ball in international rugby. Howarth quickly became the most important player on the park for the All Blacks, stepping up to slot four penalties in the first half. The Boks stayed in touch with a couple of their own. Early in the second half, the visitors broke out over halfway and looked to create a rare scoring opportunity. Unlike against the French, Stephen's cover defence was up to the task as he took care of Hennie le Roux, then Graeme came across to bundle winger James Small into touch. A few minutes later, though, it was a different story as André Joubert cruised into the line and fed big flanker Rudolf Straeuli. He smashed through Stephen like he was made of balsa wood to score the game's first try.

It took another 20 minutes of arm wrestling before the All Blacks hit back with a try of their own. Zinzan Brooke threw a cut-out ball to John Kirwan, who crossed for his thirty-fifth test try. Howarth converted to make the score 22–14, and that's the way it stayed.

If that game was a slugfest, then the next one at Athletic Park was an out-and-out war, to the point of blood being spilled in an extreme act of bitterness. As usual in Wellington, it was raining and cold when the teams met in the second test, but it started brightly as the Bachop brothers combined to open up space on the blindside to send John Timu over for the game's opening try. Brooke followed it up with his pushover try and it seemed like, all of a sudden, the All Blacks had landed a devastating two-punch combo that the Springboks would struggle to recover from. It was even more remarkable that they'd done it into the wind, too. Stephen and Graeme marshalled the backline effectively but they couldn't combine to crack the line again.

The Boks were always going to face a tough time of it going into the wind in the second half. They could only manage three penalties in total, but stayed in touch right to the end as the All Blacks won 13–9. So there it was, a series win over South Africa. A truly joyous and momentous day despite the dour rugby and wintry conditions, right? Not really.

After the All Blacks were penalised for going over the top in a ruck, le Roux saw his opportunity to gain a bit of revenge and chomped on Fitzpatrick's left ear.

The test had been marred by Springbok prop Johan le Roux deciding to have a mid-game snack on Sean Fitzpatrick. Le Roux had borne the brunt of the All Blacks' scrum dominance for the whole game and had most probably been reminded of it at every turn by the All Blacks captain. After the All Blacks were penalised for going over the top in a ruck, le Roux saw his opportunity to gain a bit of revenge and chomped on Fitzpatrick's left ear.

Le Roux was sent home and ended up with one of the longest suspensions ever handed down to a player—19 months—which, if upheld, would have ended his career. It was reduced to six on appeal and he was back playing the next season.

While the first two tests had a fair bit of drama attached despite the games themselves being relatively light on highlights, the less said about the third test, the better. It ended 18–all, on paper a worthy sequel to the epic played out at Eden Park in 1981, but in reality a snoozefest bereft of anything worth remembering. Nevertheless, it meant that the All Blacks had won the series over the old foe by two tests to nil.

The reaction, though, wasn't that of a crowd that had just witnessed a chapter worthy of enshrining in All Blacks folklore. It remained muted throughout the game, and then at the end the punters showed exactly how they felt by failing to give a standing ovation despite a sponsor's rep suggesting one during the post-match formalities. Why did that happen in 1994? Had times changed that much?

Perhaps All Blacks fans had grown used to the more exciting brand of rugby that had been regularly played against the Wallabies over the past decade. After all, the last few times they'd played the world champions had been some of the best rugby seen in a long time—a thrilling series in 1992 and highly satisfying victory the year before for the Bledisloe Cup. Maybe younger fans were puzzled at the arrival of the South Africans back on the scene; after all, they'd spent the last decade with the memory of protests and controversy and then watched the sort of rugby that was more befitting of their grandparents' generation. It's a strange one.

Less than a fortnight later, though, there would be the sort of game that is remembered as a classic. Unfortunately for the

All Blacks, they'd be on the wrong side of the result. It's the only Bledisloe Cup test to have been played on a Wednesday night, and like the ear-bite test in Wellington, it would go down in history for one famous play.

The All Blacks found themselves down by a converted try after only 17 seconds, with Jason Little climbing over Howarth to catch a bomb. Stephen's defensive frailties again got exposed as Phil Kearns barged through him to score the Wallabies' second. At half-time the All Blacks had clawed it back to a slightly more doable 17–6 deficit, but this was an Australian outfit that was determined to snatch back the Bledisloe Cup at all costs.

Gregan, who'd been tracking the whole movement in the backfield, suddenly swooped in and smashed Wilson's midsection as he dived over the line, jolting the ball loose and winning the game for the Wallabies.

Marking Graeme that day was a young halfback called George Gregan. He watched on as Shane Howarth kicked another penalty then stepped through the Wallaby defensive line to close the gap right up. With five minutes to go, the score stood at 20–16.

Jeff Wilson, who'd been recalled at the expense of John Kirwan after the Springbok series win (a move that prompted Kirwan to say that Laurie Mains had 'lost the plot'), got a pass on the Wallabies' 40-metre line, stepped inside two defenders, then turned David Campese into a human turnstile as he sped past, on course to surely win the game for the All Blacks. Gregan, who'd been tracking the whole movement in the backfield, suddenly swooped in and smashed Wilson's midsection as he dived over the line, jolting the ball loose and winning the game for the Wallabies.

Even the most one-eyed All Blacks fan could admit they'd just seen an epic test match with perhaps the most memorable finish in Bledisloe Cup history. But for Stephen Bachop, it was to be the last time he pulled on the All Blacks jersey. The Bachop brothers' All Blacks time together had lasted four tests, three out-and-out battles with the Springboks and a heartbreak against the Wallabies. But they weren't done with test rugby, not by a long shot.

First, there was the matter of another one of the many games the Bachop brothers played against one another. Since Stephen's move to Otago, he and Graeme would square off regularly when the two powerhouse southern unions met in the National Provincial Championship. One of the most famous matches between the two sides occurred in 1994, as Canterbury had wrested the Ranfurly Shield off Waikato and now put it on the line in front of a capacity crowd at Lancaster Park.

This wasn't going to eventuate into a classic brother versus brother showdown, unfortunately. Graeme's contribution was limited to temporarily stifling the fired-up Otago forwards from scoring when he held up a charge over the line. Not long after Jamie Joseph did smash his way over, Graeme left the field injured. Nevertheless, this game is notable for being Stephen's turn to steal the limelight, guiding the handy Otago team full of young uni students and grizzled veterans to lead the Shield holders at half-time. He'd got in on the scoring action too, placing a perfectly weighted left-footed kick into Canterbury's 22 that evaded both Otago winger Paul Cooke and Canterbury's Paula Bale, then bounced straight back into his hands for him to effortlessly dive over in the corner.

However, the player marking him was having a good game of his own. In fact, 21-year-old Andrew Mehrtens was having a great season for Canterbury, and his name was definitely on the minds of those looking forward to the next year's World Cup.

After a wildly entertaining 79 minutes, Otago found themselves up 20–19 as time expired, and Mehrtens drove them into their own 22 for a defensive lineout. A decent take and clearance may well have held that slim lead until time expired, and Stephen dropped back into his own in-goal to await the pass from Stu Forster. Unfortunately, it was perhaps the worst pass the All Blacks halfback ever threw; instead of going into Stephen's hands it dribbled woefully across the goal line to be forced dead for a five-metre scrum to Canterbury.

Then, like in Sydney, the drama came. Canterbury shifted the ball to midfield. Stephen made a tackle on Mark Mayerhofler and the ball came loose at the ruck. Otago skipper David Latta, who had earlier unselfishly passed to Forster for what would have been the winning try, dived on it. The problem, according to referee Colin Hawke, is that the ball wasn't loose enough and Latta was pinged for the most important penalty of his life. Mehrtens teed the ball up only inches away from an almost catatonic Latta, lying prostrate on the turf as the realisation of what he'd done sank in.

The new wonderkid of New Zealand rugby calmly split the posts with the penalty. Otago's Ranfurly Shield drought had started in 1957, and it would continue until 2013—long after every single player involved in this game was well and truly retired. Mehrtens' display heralded his arrival as an All Black in waiting; indeed, once the next season came around he would make his debut and then play a starring role at the 1995 World Cup on the way to a record-breaking career in test rugby.

It helped no end in 1995 that Mehrtens had a halfback giving him the ball who had the best year of his entire career, and would end the year with no doubt that he was the best in the world at his position. While Stephen was gone, Graeme was now solidly the first choice in the number 9 jersey, and scored a try in the All Blacks' only lead-up test to the World Cup against Canada at Eden Park. It was a new-look side with three new players only a month out from the first pool game, which, in this day and age, would be seen as absolute madness. Especially considering that Josh Kronfeld, Mehrtens and Glen Osborne were coming into the most vital positions in the team at openside, first five and fullback.

It was a new-look side with three new players only a month out from the first pool game, which, in this day and age, would be seen as absolute madness.

In a cruel bit of marketing foolery, Caltex New Zealand was distributing figurines of the All Blacks World Cup squad from their gas stations, dubbed the 'Small Blacks'—but they'd launched them well before the side had been named. Whoever was in charge of the campaign had mostly relied on what the team had been the year before. Stephen and the also-out-of-favour Shane Howarth (who would feel most unlucky considering he'd scored every single point in the All Blacks' last two tests) found themselves in the awkward position of being part of the set, while the new caps and the about-to-be-recalled Jonah Lomu were conspicuously absent.

With the exception of the hiding they gave Japan in the pool stage, Graeme started and finished every match at the World Cup for the All Blacks. His finest moment, like more than a few others, came in their demolition of England in the semi-final at Cape Town. It was here that he threw probably the most notable pass of his life—even though it more than slightly missed its mark and bounced up into the hands of the player it was intended for.

That player, of course, was Lomu. Two minutes into the game Graeme darted around the side of a ruck and floated a ball over the top of Osborne to Lomu's wing, and the winger scored the stand-out try of his career by bulldozing over the top of English fullback Mike Catt to cross the line. His name was immortalised by Keith Quinn's call: 'Bachop again, New Zealand maintaining possession . . . he goes WIDE to Lomu . . . he's got the bounce, HE'S HANDED OFF HIS OPPOSITE, LOMU . . . OH, OH . . .' Graeme also scored one of the All Blacks' six tries that day. He finished the game how he started it: after picking off an English pass, he immediately looked for the quickest way to get the ball to Lomu, who then ran 50 metres through the English defenders for his fourth try.

After the final loss to the Springboks, the All Blacks returned to face the Wallabies in two tests for the Bledisloe Cup. Now that Lomu, the closest thing to a thermonuclear weapon that a rugby team arsenal could possess, had returned, the matches were predicted to be walkovers. The first at Eden Park ended 28–16, but in reality could have gone either way had it not been for a late try and a couple of dropped goals by Mehrtens. The next game, in Sydney, was a chance to make up for what happened in 1994.

First off, there was no George Gregan to deal with. Graeme's modus operandi was to get the ball out as fast as possible—the All Blacks backs were under strict instructions under the Sydney sun to get the ball to Lomu. They reaped the benefits of this by giving Lomu enough space to charge down the wing and set up Frank Bunce for the opening try, then get himself one in the second half. Fittingly, the last All Blacks try was scored by Wilson, who made an extravagant dive into the corner to help bury the demons of his fumble the year before.

The Bledisloe Cup was back in New Zealand, which somewhat made up for the World Cup disappointment. But the 34–23 win was the last-ever appearance for the star player of the 1995 All Blacks. After 31 tests, the advent of professionalism was going to see the rules tightened around just who could play for the All Blacks, and that meant Graeme's impending contract in Japan would prohibit adding to that total.

While this may seem like par for the course these days, this was new territory for the All Blacks. During the World Cup, flanker Kevin Schuler was picked despite not having played in New Zealand for several seasons, and many others over the past decades had gone to Italy and France for so-called amateur contracts that in reality were simply laying the foundations for the game to ultimately turn pro. The week leading up to the second Bledisloe test saw a challenge from a private consortium, the World Rugby Corporation, which might well have seen the world's leading players abandon what we know as test rugby. It was staved off at the last minute by some deft boardroom manoeuvring, but the NZRU knew that ring-fencing their talent pool was the only way that the game in New Zealand would survive the new era.

It essentially came down to: you're either in or you're out. Graeme's contract with Sanix was guaranteeing him good money, so he was out.

Out of the All Blacks, that is. Out of test rugby? Not quite.

While Graeme headed to the land of the rising sun, the next few seasons saw the first saplings of professionalism take shape, firstly in the form of Super 12. Instead of simply playing where they lived, the best players in the country were redistributed where they were needed. Stephen started the inaugural 1996 season with the Highlanders. However, the dearth of talent in the first-five position faced by the struggling Hurricanes meant that he moved north to join a motley bunch of rising stars, nearly men and assorted offcuts.

Stephen found himself in the form of his life, commanding a backline containing a young centre called Tana Umaga.

They'd only won three games in their first season. No one was expecting anything out of the Hurricanes at all in 1997, except maybe a couple more spectacular tries to recent All Black Christian Cullen.

Those that trekked along to Athletic Park that year definitely saw a few of those. However, they got to see a truckload more through a team that suddenly had their power cable seemingly plugged in and running on high voltage. Under the coaching of former All Black Frank Oliver, the Hurricanes committed themselves to playing a high-tempo game that epitomised the early, carefree years of the Super 12. Stephen found himself in the form of his life, commanding a backline containing a young centre called Tana Umaga.

The Hurricanes became the hottest ticket in town. In May of that year they played the Blues at Eden Park in what is probably the greatest Super Rugby game of all time, coming back from 35–16 down in the second half to only just get pipped 45–42 by the All Blacks-stacked defending champions. It ensured that the Hurricanes now had a reputation for being the entertaining underdogs, one that somehow sticks with them despite the fact that they aren't exactly short of All Blacks talent these days.

The team ended up making the semi-finals, after selling out Athletic Park for their last home game, but were undone by the clinical Brumbies in Canberra. Stephen's career had rebounded after the disappointment of being cut loose by the All Blacks, and he decided to sign on to play provincial rugby with a new amalgamation team called the Central Vikings later that year.

On paper, the Central Vikings concept made sense. The Hawke's Bay and Manawatu unions were mired in the National Provincial Championship second division, and needed a way to break back into the big time to recapture their glory days. Stephen found himself surrounded by some familiar faces from the Hurricanes' breakout year, including Cullen, with Frank Oliver retained as coach. Unfortunately, this was a merger between two teams that had traditionally hated one another for their entire existences, so the running of the venture was fraught with difficulty from day one.

It didn't affect the on-field performance, at least not at first. The Vikings, dressed in gaudy orange and blue jerseys that had no connection whatsoever to the unions they represented, coasted past their second-division rivals and looked destined to break into the first division and maybe even challenge Wellington as the major player in the Hurricanes region.

The NZRU had other ideas. Because the two unions hadn't officially merged, it was decreed that the Vikings couldn't be promoted, and the news of that decision came through the week the team was supposed to play in the second-division final against Northland. It's not too much of a stretch to say that rendering the game meaningless contributed quite a bit to the 63–10 scoreline going in Northland's favour.

It meant that Stephen, like his brother before him, looked offshore for opportunities. Stephen was about to pull on the blue jersey of Samoa again.

Stephen saw out the next year with the Hurricanes and Vikings; however, the Super 12 season brought with it expectations that the Canes couldn't live up to. It turned out that 1997 was a blip of success rather than a new dawn, and the sun wouldn't start to rise on that franchise until well into the new century. As for the Vikings, Cullen decided to shift to Wellington, and the inability to gain promotion coupled with some severe financial troubles doomed the team's future. In a cruel twist, they went through the season unbeaten, winning the second division before splitting back up into the former entities and going into the history books as an interesting bit of trivia.

It meant that Stephen, like his brother before him, looked offshore for opportunities. By now, the English Premiership had emerged as a viable option for ex-All Blacks like himself, and he signed on at London Irish. The UK was a handy place to be, because that's where the next Rugby World Cup was to be held, and the team that he made his test debut for was still very much interested in having him on board. Stephen was about to pull on the blue jersey of Samoa again.

Meanwhile, Graeme's Japanese experience was rolling along nicely. At the start of 1996, new All Blacks coach John Hart had argued the case to make an exemption for Graeme to be selected for the side despite playing overseas, and the call was certainly supported by the public because of his outstanding World Cup form in 1995. However, it became clear reasonably quickly that Graeme's successor Justin Marshall was more than up to the task, so the NZRU was justified in holding firm against Hart's wishes and the matter was forgotten.

But, after four years there, Graeme now qualified as a residential player and was eligible to represent Japan at test level. Rugby's eligibility laws were still as flimsy as ever, so he too would now go to a World Cup for another nation. Just to make things more interesting, Samoa and Japan were in the same pool.

When it came time for the two sides to meet in what was the opening match for both in the tournament, the Bachop brothers weren't the only former All Blacks to take the field. Jamie Joseph started at openside for Japan, while Inga Tuigamala lined up at second five and Pat Lam at number 8 for Samoa. To complete the All Blacks connection, the Japanese side was captained by Andrew McCormick, son of legendary former fullback Fergie.

Unlike the Bachops' Ranfurly Shield clash in Christchurch five years previously, the game didn't eventuate into a tense match at all, and Stephen got the last laugh this time as Samoa rolled over Japan 43–9 at the Racecourse Ground in Wrexham. It was another poor tournament showing by the Japanese, and it'd be another 16 years until their first win at a World Cup.

For the Samoans, though, it was the start of another World Cup to remember. The upset of Wales in 1991 was still fresh in the memories of everyone and, as fate would have it, they would repeat the fixture in their next match. This time it would be played at Cardiff's brand-new Millennium Stadium in front of 73,000 people. It would end up being probably the finest game of Stephen's career.

There was yet another adventure in eligibility, with yet another former All Black involved. Shane Howarth, whose career since had seen him play league and then shift to the UK, started at fullback for Wales. Samoa were coached by Bryan Williams, and Wales by future All Blacks coach Graham Henry.

The Irish commentator mistakenly called him 'Bishop', then completely butchered fullback Silao Leaegailesolo's name as he burst through the line.

After finding themselves up 12–3 after 20 minutes, it looked as though the Welsh were on track to avenge their shock loss. After all, they were tournament hosts and hadn't built the magnificent stadium so they could lose to a minnow team from the Pacific Islands. Then the wheels started to fall off when they tossed a long lineout throw straight into the arms of Lio Falaniko, who flopped over the line for an easy try. Later in the half, Stephen moved the ball out from an attacking scrum to the Samoan backline. The Irish commentator mistakenly called him 'Bishop', then completely butchered fullback Silao Leaegailesolo's name as he burst through the line. Leaegailesolo popped a pass back to Stephen, who scored under the posts just in time for the caller to get his name right.

Five minutes later, and he was in on the action again. Scott

Quinnell made a complete mess of a pass from the back of his scrum to Howarth, and Stephen scooped up the loose ball to scoot 50 metres to score and put Samoa into the lead. The Welsh weren't done gift-wrapping opportunities, though. Just after half-time Neil Jenkins floated a perfect pass for Pat Lam to pick off and run back 70 metres. Samoa were in a generous mood themselves, handing the Welsh two penalty tries.

After 65 minutes, the 31–all deadlock was broken when Leaegailesolo dived over for his second try in the corner to take the lead. From then on, they had to grimly hang on as the Welsh threw everything at their line. A string of penalties at the end meant that Wales had every chance to pull level and earn a remarkable draw. But it wasn't to be. The ball was held up, the final whistle blew and history repeated itself—Wales had been upset in a World Cup by Samoa.

Stephen had played a leading hand in both games, eight years apart. In another eerie coincidence, they faced Scotland in their knockout game, just like they'd done in 1991. Just like in 1991, they lost. Stephen Bachop's long and winding test career was over, with his brother's coming to an end as well the week before as Japan were beaten by Argentina.

Graeme returned to play for Sanix, and a year later found himself lining up in Tokyo against the All Blacks in a Pacific Rim Barbarians side—which in reality was just a bunch of former New Zealand players plying their trade in Japan. His association with the All Blacks had ended in the same place it had started. Stephen saw out his contract at London Irish, and returned home to New Zealand.

It wasn't long until the Bachop name was mentioned repeatedly again to New Zealand rugby fans. Aaron and Nathan Mauger, destined to be All Blacks brothers themselves, were nephews of Stephen and Graeme—a fact that was often repeated during their Super Rugby and international careers. Nowadays, you'll hear it again. Jackson Garden-Bachop, Stephen's son, plays for Wellington and the Hurricanes, and had a stint playing for the Melbourne Rebels. Like his old man, he's a first five.

The Bachop brothers' combined career spanned 13 years and three test-playing nations. They played against each other five times for Otago and Canterbury, then became the first brothers to oppose each other during a Rugby World Cup match.

Of course, you can't do that any more. Eligibility rules are now so tight players are locked in to playing for one team for the rest of their lives as soon as they pull on a jersey. That's what makes the Bachop brothers' story unique.

LEFT TOP: Xavier Rush in 1998. He and sister Annaleah both wore the black jersey, representing New Zealand on the same field on the same day. **PHOTOSPORT**

LEFT BELOW: Annaleah Rush throws a quickfire pass during a Women's Rugby World Cup match in 2002. **PHOTOSPORT/PEP MORATA**

RIGHT: Niall Williams and her brother Sonny Bill both represented New Zealand at the 2016 Olympic Games. **PHOTOSPORT/ANDREW CORNAGA**

SISTER ACT

THE YEAR 2018 SAW QUITE a bit of chest-beating from New Zealand Rugby about the series of double-header matches between both the All Blacks and Wallabies, as well as the Black Ferns and Wallaroos. The women's sides, so often overlooked in the national calculations, were finally getting to share the spotlight with their male counterparts. The matches took place at ANZ Stadium in Sydney, as well as at Eden Park—leading many to believe that it was the first time such a fixture had been arranged.

Except it wasn't. Twenty years previously, the newly christened Black Ferns (up until then they had been known only as the New Zealand Women's Rugby team) played before the Bledisloe Cup test at the Sydney Football Stadium. The day contained a bit of history that hasn't been repeated since.

By the time the double-header happened, Annaleah Rush had been in the women's side for two years. So far she'd never lost in a black jersey, had won the first of five World Cups the team would claim over the next two decades, and as the team's goal kicker had racked up 134 points in 10 tests. All of that made the impending victory her team would have over their Australian rivals not really anything out of the ordinary. What was unique about when she played on 28 August 1998 in Sydney is that her brother Xavier was getting ready to play for the All Blacks on the same field straight afterwards.

They'd grown up in Auckland, but Annaleah eventually represented Otago after leaving school. Xavier's time in the Sacred Heart first XV had put him on track to represent Auckland and the Blues, but the timing of his career meant that he was called up probably far too soon.

While the women's team had triumphantly won their World Cup in May of that year, 1998 was the year that the All Blacks were a disaster (see the Brooke brothers' chapter). Retirements, injuries and sheer desperation from coach John Hart saw Xavier get a call-up for the third Bledisloe Cup test of the year. The selection wasn't Xavier's fault: Hart was simply needing something, anything, to go his way in the last match of a season that had already seen four losses in a row.

The 21-year-old was set to start at number 8. He could've looked to his sister for inspiration, because out on the park, centre Annaleah had scored a try and kicked a conversion in her side's 27–3 win.

The All Blacks couldn't match their feat. Not even after the reliable Wallabies fullback Matt Burke couldn't hit the side of a barn with his goal kicks, leading to John Eales taking over in the second half. The 19–14 loss was another bitter pill to swallow for New Zealand rugby fans, and Xavier was right in the middle of it after dropping a bomb on the All Blacks' 10-metre line that led directly to the match-winning try for the Wallabies.

So far, Xavier and Annaleah Rush are the only brother and sister to play test rugby for New Zealand at the same venue. But it's not the only time it's happened in a black jersey on the world stage. There's an awful lot you can say about Sonny Bill Williams, but this fact is another feature of his exceptional career: he and sister Niall have played on the same field a few times for the All

Blacks and Black Ferns Sevens teams. As in the case of Annaleah and Xavier, it's the sister who has had more success in these outings.

A gold medal should have been the main priority for 2016, a year with nothing comparatively important on for the All Blacks. But instead of giving it their full support, key players started making themselves unavailable.

Both Sonny Bill and Niall were picked to represent New Zealand at the 2016 Olympics in Rio de Janeiro, which was the first time rugby had been a part of the Games in 92 years. Hopes were high for the men; at least, they were initially when it was presumed that the Sevens side would be able to have their pick of whichever All Blacks they wanted for the tournament. A gold medal should have been the main priority for 2016, a year with nothing comparatively important on for the All Blacks. But instead of giving it their full support, key players started making themselves unavailable.

Sonny Bill stayed loyal to his goal of making the Games, but by the time he arrived the team basically looked like the same one that played at all the regular Sevens World Series tournaments. It didn't help that he got injured in the first game, a shock loss to Japan. His Achilles tendon tear meant that he was out for the rest of the tournament and a good chunk of the season as well. The men's side capitulated to finish fifth overall.

Meanwhile, the women's team that Niall had been selected

for had no such problems getting the players they wanted. Like Kayla McAlister, sister of former All Black Luke, and also a former top netballer. Portia Woodman, another former netballer and daughter of All Black Kawhena. Gayle Broughton, Theresa Fitzpatrick, Ruby Tui and Tyla Nathan-Wong, all key cogs in a team that would go on to dominate the sport in coming years.

At the Olympics, though, they came up against a stacked Australian team in the gold-medal match. You could make a case for this showdown as the jolt that sent the Black Ferns Sevens side to the height of popular consciousness in New Zealand sport—after this they became appointment viewing at any tournament they played. Ultimately, though, it was a loss. The 24–17 result still meant that the women could boast a silver medal, New Zealand's first ever in Olympic rugby.

Sonny Bill hasn't played for the Sevens team since, although with him you never know if that might change. He returned to Super Rugby and the All Blacks, and in 2017 became the third All Black to be sent off in a test match after Cyril Brownlie and Colin Meads—two other All Blacks brothers. Niall continues to be an integral part of the Black Ferns Sevens, who by the start of 2019 had avenged their Olympic loss by beating Australia in the Commonwealth Games gold-medal match and had established a six-tournament win streak.

The Sevens programme can boast even more than just Sonny Bill and Niall Williams as a family connection. Stacey and Beaudein Waaka, Terina and Isaac Te Tamaki and Jordon and Joe Webber have also entered the books as Silver Ferns Sevens siblings.

Xavier Rush was dropped after the loss to the Wallabies, and seemed destined to be a one-test All Black. However, in one of the more remarkable comebacks in the professional era, six years of hard slog at the Blues and Auckland saw him recalled in 2004 to play seven more tests, including a highly satisfying series win against the newly crowned world-champion England side.

Annaleah Rush's career after the game in Sydney didn't contain as many tests as she probably would have liked, but that's more to do with the women's sides not getting as many games as the men, than any lack of ability. In all, she played 20 tests, won two World Cups and finished her career as the top scorer for the team at the time with 152 points.

The Black Ferns, for the foreseeable future, will play double-headers with the All Blacks. The Black Ferns Sevens routinely take the field on the same day as their All Blacks Sevens counterparts. Given the increasing number of girls picking up rugby balls across Aotearoa, the sight of a sister and brother wearing a black jersey on the same day again isn't a matter of if, but when.

Akira (left) and Rieko Ioane, part of the new breed of All Blacks brothers.
PHOTOSPORT/ANTHONY AU-YEUNG

THE MODERN ERA

THE DEANS FAMILY NAME HAS a long association with both Canterbury and New Zealand rugby. Oh, and also Australian rugby, thanks to Robbie Deans' highly publicised shift over the ditch after missing out on the All Blacks coaching job in 2007. It was a big deal, made into a personal battle with Graham Henry, not to mention that it prompted an unpeeling of the festering scab that holds in the provincial angst between Canterbury and the rest of the country.

In fact, all of Robbie's very successful career as a coach is a big deal, which is why it's often overlooked that he was also a player of some remarkable talent in the early 1980s. He had the misfortune of having a career that coincided with considerable depth in the fullback position for the All Blacks, though. His breakthrough came on the 1983 tour to the UK, which remains the All Blacks' worst-ever return in terms of results over there. The test with Scotland was drawn and the one against England lost. Robbie survived the fallout from that to make the side that toured Australia in 1984, but ultimately it wasn't going to be any performances in an All Blacks jersey that would cost him his spot.

He eventually fell out of favour due to his involvement with the Cavaliers tour. By the end of 1986, John Gallagher had locked down the fullback spot for the next four seasons, which meant he got to sit at the back of one of the most dominant teams of all time. Robbie then turned to coaching after he retired from playing, first masterminding Canterbury's rise to the top of the provincial ranks then turning the Crusaders into the dynastic force that has dominated Super Rugby for the past two decades. In 2001, he was appointed assistant All Blacks coach with John Mitchell, a reign which didn't exactly leave either man looking the best after the 2003 World Cup semi-final exit. Since then, he went on to coach the Wallabies, and now is in charge of the Panasonic Wyld Knights in Japan. Stories of his coaching influence are revealing when you talk to the players he's mentored—Robbie is a man who certainly knows how to get the balance right when it comes to dealing with them.

Before one game against the Coca-Cola Red Sparks in the Japanese Top League, Robbie invited the coaching staff of the bottom-ranked team to have a discussion about what they could do better and how he could help.

Of course, he wasn't the first Robert Deans to play for the All Blacks—Great-uncle Bob was the man at the centre of the Original All Blacks controversy against Wales. In a perfect world, Robbie would have scored a try against the Welsh all those years later, but the honour of doing that went to his brother.

Bruce Deans was the Canterbury halfback that eventually got a shot at the All Blacks after David Kirk's sudden retirement to take up a Rhodes Scholarship. He'd watched on for the entire World Cup as Kirk captained the side to glory, and eventually got his first game in the tour to Japan at the end of that year. He made it count, scoring a hat-trick against the Japanese, before gaining some revenge for his family by scoring tries in consecutive tests as the All Blacks destroyed Wales in a two-test series in 1988. He looked set to entrench himself as the halfback for the next World

Cup, but the Welsh curse struck the Deans family again in 1989. Bruce injured himself in the lead-up to the test match that year in Cardiff, and Graeme Bachop was brought in as his replacement. As you can read in the Bachop brothers' chapter, that was the end of the road for Bruce.

The man who initially replaced Robbie Deans in the Baby Blacks team that played without any of the Cavaliers players was then-Auckland fullback Greg Cooper. Despite confidently kicking a dropped goal in his first test win, the reality that the Cavaliers ban was little more than a slap on the wrist hit home when he was replaced by Kieran Crowley by the time the All Blacks toured France. Greg shifted south to Otago after that, which paid off handsomely after the 1991 World Cup clean-out by Laurie Mains.

Otago man Mains went with the guys he knew, which meant that Greg got a call-up to play his fourth test six years after playing his third. It was almost the same time between drinks for his younger brother, Matt.

Matt Cooper had originally gone on the 1987 end-of-year tour to Japan, but wasn't picked again until the 1992 series. Unfortunately, it came at the expense of his brother—Greg paid the price for a lacklustre All Blacks 24–21 win over Ireland in Dunedin that ended his All Blacks career. It was only the second time an All Black had replaced his own brother, after Stan Meads took over from Colin in 1962.

While it must have made Christmas at the Cooper household a bit awkward that year, Mains was proved to be right. Matt ended the next test as the new record-holder for points on debut as an All Black, scoring 23 and locking himself in the team for the next two seasons. He would, like his brother, become a victim of another poor team performance in 1994—dropped after the series loss to France. He did, however, reappear in a couple of tour games on the triumphant 1996 tour to South Africa.

But the one moment that Greg Cooper is unfortunately associated with didn't come in an All Blacks jersey. Matt's provincial career had seen him land in Waikato, after starting out in their home province of Hawke's Bay. Their NPC final that year was against Greg's Otago team. Like the Bachops, they spent more games playing against rather than alongside one another.

That day at Rugby Park saw probably the most blatant act of foul play ever caught on camera in a rugby match in New Zealand. After only 15 minutes of play, All Blacks prop Richard Loe grabbed hold of Greg's face and brutally gouged his eye. It probably would have escaped much attention, had it not been for TVNZ journalist Richard Becht going back and studying the different angles of the incident and then making sure it made the news for the following week. Loe was suspended for nine months after Kevin Skinner, a man who clearly felt that intimidating your opponent was far more fair when you punched them in the face, threatened to return his All Blacks test tie if appropriate action wasn't taken.

That day at Rugby Park saw probably the most blatant act of foul play ever caught on camera in a rugby match in New Zealand.

Matt and Greg both went on to take advantage of the new broadcasting arrangement with Sky TV. They both had stints as analysts before Greg moved into coaching, first with Otago and then the Highlanders; these days he's with the amazingly named Mitsubishi DynaBoars club in Japan.

Matt's teammates during his time at Waikato included Rob and Steve Gordon, two locks who would become All Blacks in the early '90s. When they were picked to tour France in 1990, along with Gary and AJ Whetton, they became the first two sets of brothers to be picked in the All Blacks since the Meads and Clarkes back in 1963–64.

While Rob's career lasted only three tour matches, Steve eventually played two tests at the end of 1993 against Scotland and England. The test in Edinburgh was a hiding and notable for Jeff Wilson's stunning three-try debut, but the next at Twickenham was a shock 15–9 loss.

Rob does have one unique claim to fame, though. Against Southland in 1990 he scored five tries in a 75–11 Waikato win, which remains an NPC first-division record. He also moved to Japan in the late '90s and, like Graeme Bachop, was selected for their World Cup team in 1999. While he didn't play any tests for the All Blacks, he had 17 for the Brave Blossoms.

The connections continue for the next set of brothers that played for the All Blacks, in 2001. Aaron and Nathan Mauger are the nephews of the Bachop brothers, and followed in Graeme's footsteps to carve out careers with Canterbury. However, if there was ever a modern case for one brother's All Black status overshadowing the other's, this is it.

Aaron played 45 tests over six seasons, including going to two World Cups and even captaining the side once. Nathan's entire time on the field was two games in the space of a week, and it was over before Aaron had even made his debut.

Two games against Ireland A and Scotland A were as good

as it got for Nathan, who spent the rest of the tour watching his brother and the rest of the test side convincingly beat their full international opponents in the UK, then almost lose against Argentina. He can boast, though, that he was part of the all-conquering Crusaders side for the 2003–04 seasons.

Aaron was part of John Mitchell and Robbie Deans' ill-fated 2003 World Cup side, and spent the next few years as part of an All Blacks side that was beginning to feel the weight of a nation deprived of World Cup glory. He formed a solid midfield partnership with Tana Umaga as the All Blacks saw off the woefully outgunned 2005 British & Irish Lions side that left New Zealand on the back of a 3–0 series loss, although he conceded his third-test spot to Luke McAlister, the man who would be the main competition for his jersey throughout his career.

Ultimately, it was McAlister that ended up playing in what turned out to be the most important defeat of the decade for the All Blacks. The quarter-final loss to France in Cardiff at the 2007 World Cup led to a complete overhaul in the midfield—from then on it would be the celebrated combination of Conrad Smith and Ma'a Nonu for the better part of the next eight seasons. Aaron's international career ended, and he left to play in England for Leicester.

In that Lions series, a piece of All Blacks history that probably will never be repeated took place. Nelson Bays winger Rico Gear became the last All Black to be picked from a second-division provincial side. But this wasn't like the old-school tales of a provincial battler finally getting a call-up after grafting away in the rural fields of New Zealand—it was more like one of the realities of being a modern, professional player having to take the opportunities presented to him. Originally from Gisborne, Gear had made his test debut the year before playing out of North Harbour. Nelson Bays was already his fourth province, after stints with Auckland and Bay of Plenty, as well as playing for the Crusaders and Blues. He'd also won a Commonwealth Games Sevens gold medal in 1998.

Rico moved south in order to qualify to play for the Crusaders, as regulations had tightened up meaning fewer players from outside the franchise region were allowed in each Super Rugby team. It was a smart move; he scored a record 15 tries in the 2005 Super Rugby season, and was ushered back into a crowded All Blacks wing picture that included Doug Howlett, Sitiveni Sivivatu, Joe Rokocoko and Mils Muliaina when he wasn't being picked at fullback.

This wealth of talent meant that we probably saw far less of Rico Gear than if he'd played for any other test nation. It's a problem shared by many All Blacks wingers. In all, Rico finished with an excellent strike rate of 11 tries from 19 tests, but he was always seen as a second option to the prolific Rokocoko. Like Aaron Mauger, he shifted overseas at the end of the 2007 season, after not making the World Cup squad.

> **This wealth of talent meant that we probably saw far less of Rico Gear than if he'd played for any other test nation.**

It meant that he wasn't around for the next season, when his brother Hosea burst onto the scene. He too has a provincial claim to fame, by representing the boys' home province of Poverty Bay while still a high-school student. Like Rico, he moved to

Wellington in the hopes of securing a Super Rugby spot.

Hosea grafted away in a Hurricanes team that underperformed throughout the 2000s, before breaking into the All Blacks on the back of a 14-try NPC season for Wellington in 2008. Again, like his brother, he found himself competing with Sivivatu, Rokocoko, his Hurricane teammate Cory Jane, and Zac Guildford for a test spot. It seemed like his test career may have just been a blip on the All Blacks story, except for his stunning form on the 2010 Grand Slam tour.

'Grand Slam' is a phrase that gets bandied about with probably way too much meaning on it for the All Blacks. The reason it took them 73 years of trying before they finally achieved the task of beating England, Ireland, Scotland and Wales on one tour has more to do with off-field impediments (Scotland refusing to play in 1924, the Irish leg being cancelled in 1967, nothing scheduled during the late '80s). But a player scoring tries in each test is one record that hasn't yet been achieved by an All Black.

Hosea Gear can claim he's got the closest, at least. He scored a contentious try against England at Twickenham, then two each against Scotland and Wales—only just missing out on one in Dublin. He did eventually get a try against Ireland two years later when they were massacred by the All Blacks 60–0 in Hamilton.

He can also boast that he was part of the 2011 World Cup-winning squad. However, having been brought in as a late injury replacement, he never made it into any of the match-day 22s. The arrival of Julian Savea in 2012 heralded the end of another glorious but brief All Blacks winger career for the Gear family, with Hosea departing to play in France at the end of the season.

The man who eventually replaced Savea as the All Blacks' strike winger, Rieko Ioane, made his debut in 2017 against the

British & Irish Lions. By the end of the year, his brother Akira had joined him in the team, but so far his All Blacks career has been one tour game against a French XV.

While the Gear and Ioane brothers made a few headlines due to their scoring abilities, the same can't be said of Hawke's Bay lock Bryn Evans. It's fair to say he hadn't really made any at all before he was picked to play against France in 2009, eventually coming off the bench to replace Isaac Ross late in the shock 27–22 loss in Dunedin. He repeated the process a week later in Wellington, and at least managed to be part of a 14–10 win. After that, he returned to Hawke's Bay and eventually the Hurricanes, but saw barely any game time behind Jason Eaton and Jeremy Thrush.

While that really was an out-of-the-blue All Blacks career, his younger brother Gareth has had a far more traditional rise to fame. His form with the Highlanders saw him touted as a future All Blacks loose forward early on, and then an outstanding season after moving to the Hurricanes in 2018 meant that goal was likely to happen sooner or later.

Thanks to Steve Hansen picking basically every decent player on the Japanese leg of the end-of-year tour, it ended up being a case of 'sooner'. Gareth, along with seven other debutants, played against Japan in Tokyo in an entertaining 69–31 win. As is now the traditional way for fringe players, Gareth will probably have to wait until the post-World Cup clean-out for a chance to establish himself as a more long-term All Black.

There were nine years, four months and 14 days between the international careers of Bryn and Gareth Evans. At present, they are the most recent set of brothers to play for the All Blacks.

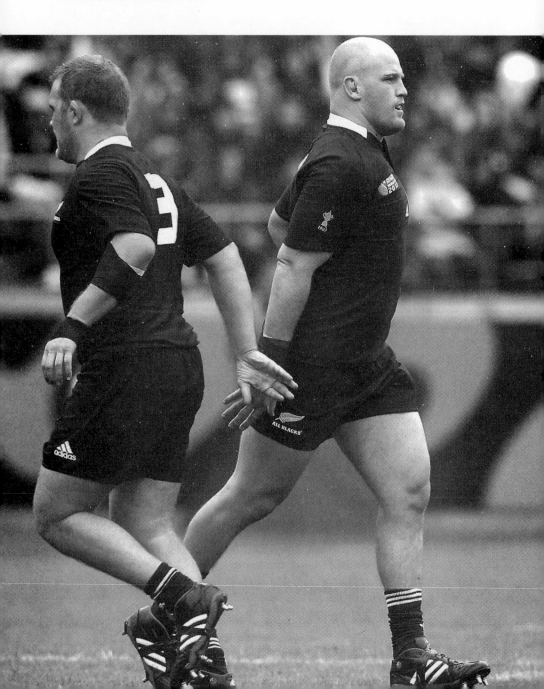

LEFT: Owen (left) and Ben Franks at the 2011 Rugby World Cup. Along with the Whitelocks, the brothers have played a key role in the All Blacks' success over the past decade. PHOTOSPORT/GRANT DOWN

RIGHT: Samuel (left) and Luke Whitelock at an All Blacks training session in mid-2018. PHOTOSPORT/ANDREW CORNAGA

THE FRANKS
AND WHITELOCKS

THERE MIGHT HAVE BEEN A certain point, probably around 50 or 60 tests, when the rest of the All Blacks might have thought about giving Owen Franks a hard time about not scoring a try in a test match. There might have been a certain point, too, when test centurion Samuel Whitelock might have thought about hassling his brothers for playing about as much rugby for the All Blacks as he would routinely forget over the course of a single season.

Key word there is 'might'. The Whitelock brothers, all four of them, are about as close to a breeding programme as New Zealand Rugby could get. Although Adam never made it to the All Blacks, he appeared 55 times for the Crusaders and played a season for the All Blacks Sevens. George's career had the misfortune of coinciding with that of Richie McCaw, but Luke is held in such high regard by the All Blacks coaching staff that he was promoted to captain in only his second game.

It's probably unlikely that anyone would seriously jibe Franks, a man so renowned for strength that he once bench-pressed a hotel bed with a sleeping teammate in it. But one man who might do is his brother Ben—after all, it only took him one test to get off the mark in terms of try-scoring. That test in New Plymouth, in June 2010, was a big night for both the Franks and Whitelock families. It was the debut of one of each of the brothers, and would be the start of their names being a regular part of the All Blacks team.

This was a long time before Ireland turned into the force that would beat the All Blacks twice in three years, though. While they had the talent of Brian O'Driscoll, Rob Kearney and Ronan O'Gara, those players had little in the way of help from a team of guys that would struggle to make a Super Rugby squad. Owen and Ben Franks started the game as the two All Blacks props. It was the first time that two brothers had started since Zinzan and Robin Brooke at Twickenham in 1997. Samuel Whitelock was on the bench, and around 25,000 were in for a test that was the second All Blacks game to be played at the recently refurbished Yarrow Stadium.

While Ben had played for the All Blacks already on a rare tour game against Munster in 2008, Owen had made his test debut in 2009. Not that many people will remember it, because it's gone down as one of the worst tests, aesthetically at least, in recent All Blacks history. Italy came to tour New Zealand and played their first test at the old Lancaster Park, by then known as AMI Stadium. It was a dour brute of a game to watch.

They eventually triumphed over an Italian side that managed to hold the All Blacks to the lowest points total they'd ever scored in 10 meetings up until that point. It was somewhat fitting; the litany of handling errors led to an above-average amount of scrums, and only three tries in a fixture where the All Blacks routinely scored over 70 points. Fitting because that's exactly what Owen Franks' career would be noted for: scrums and not scoring tries.

Also making his All Blacks debut that night was replacement flanker George Whitelock. Like Owen, he'd played his rugby for Canterbury and the Crusaders, in a loose forward trio that included McCaw and a young Kieran Read. McCaw was out for this test, meaning that Tanerau Latimer (another prodigious talent that unfortunately happened to be around the same age as the future double World Cup-winning captain) was starting at openside. Also in the side were names like Brendon Leonard, Aled de Malmanche and Lelia Masaga. On the Italian team was former Penrith Panthers, New South Wales and Kangaroos stand-off Craig Gower, who was somehow now an Italian test rugby player.

It was a nothing kick by Gower down to the promising Isaac Ross that started easily the most entertaining movement of the game.

Owen made his entry into test rugby in the fifty-ninth minute, replacing John Afoa. It was about 10 minutes after another man who became an All Blacks centurion, Tony Woodcock. Not long after that, George took the field as the All Blacks struggled to add to an unimpressive 20–6 lead.

It was a nothing kick by Gower down to the promising Isaac Ross that started easily the most entertaining movement of the game. The big lock swerved and sped up to halfway, before the ball went across the field and back for Ma'a Nonu to throw a cut-out pass to the new man wearing the number 20 jersey. George then found Owen, and then the replacement prop popped a lovely offload back to Nonu, who set up George for a clear run in to score next to the posts to make the score 27–6.

It was a perfect moment for George, scoring on test debut on his home field. Owen was the first man to congratulate him, tellingly slapping him on the silver fern emblem on his chest. It would be the last time he'd ever do that. McCaw came back in for the start of the Tri Nations series three weeks later and George was shunted out of the squad, never to return.

It was an ironic moment for Owen. He was praised for his work rate and scrummaging, but his major contribution to the game was a bit of attacking flair that would rarely be seen again in his career. He was rewarded with spots on the bench for the next couple of tests, then a start against the Springboks in Durban.

The year 2009 went down as the last time any side beat the All Blacks three times in a row. That's a stat that's likely to stay that way for quite a while, and it's fitting that the Springboks own it. Their dominance that year meant that Owen's first start was a 31–19 loss, but it didn't stop coach Graham Henry keeping him in the starting tighthead jersey for three out of the last five tests of the year. By 2010, there was no doubt over where he sat on the depth chart, and by now his brother was ready to join him in the test side.

That year again saw the South Africans win bragging rights over their New Zealand counterparts, with the Bulls triumphing over the Stormers in one of the most exciting Super Rugby finals ever played. Already thoughts were turning to the World Cup the following year, which would be held in New Zealand. George's younger brother Samuel had also risen up the ranks to be a considerable presence in the Crusaders' lineout, and was ushered into the squad to face Ireland mid-year.

Ben scored a try in the first test in New Plymouth after only 29 minutes, bashing his big frame over in the corner as the All Blacks shot out to a 38–7 lead at half-time. By the time Samuel came on, the Irish were well and truly cooked—hardly helped by the idiotic move by their number 8 Jamie Heaslip to knee McCaw in the head repeatedly in front of referee Wayne Barnes, giving him no option but to pull out a red card.

Samuel went one better than George on test debut. He scored two tries, his first coming only a matter of moments after he was injected into the game—a striding run on the end of a sweeping move that was started by his locking partner Anthony Boric. His second was even more impressive, tearing through some pathetic tackling attempts to dive over under the posts and finish the game in style for a 66–28 win.

Both men were now slotted into the All Blacks set-up for long stays. For the next while, Samuel sat on the bench while Brad Thorn and Tom Donnelly formed the locking combination. Like Owen, it was an ironic start—his first season and a half he would be spared the rigours of a starting spot. However, his career from then on opened up as he became the ultimate workhorse in the better part of a decade's worth of All Blacks test rugby.

> **Samuel went one better than George on test debut. He scored two tries, his first coming only a matter of moments after he was injected into the game.**

For Ben, though, his playing time would be almost exclusively off the bench. The Irish win was the first of 47 caps he'd earn, and only seven of them would be starts. One he suited up for and didn't even get on the field. But the time he watched an All Blacks test from the bench, he was joined by the entire nation collectively trying not to lose their minds over what became one of the most nerve-racking 80 minutes in the country's history. It was the 2011 Rugby World Cup final against France.

By now, Samuel and Owen were starting in the All Blacks tight five. Both Franks brothers had been rested for the All Blacks' pool match against Japan, but Samuel had put in an 80-minute shift. He repeated that effort against Canada, and by the time the final rolled around had played in every game of the tournament so far. He started the final alongside Thorn, while Owen formed the front row with Tony Woodcock and Keven Mealamu.

It was a game that almost everyone in New Zealand watched, and then wished they'd never have to see again. A TV showing highlights of it is probably enough to make someone change the channel, or at least put their hands over their eyes. Thankfully the highlights aren't that long: Woodcock scoring a try in the first half, then an out-of-shape Stephen Donald coming on to perform his act of redemption in the second (just why everyone thought he needed to redeem himself in the first place is pretty ridiculous anyway). But the low score contributed to the colossal collective stress that everyone was feeling. After all, this was a French team that the All Blacks had handsomely beaten in their pool match.

It was a game that almost everyone in New Zealand watched, and then wished they'd never have to see again.

Owen and Samuel had their work cut out for them in the tight; the French had little intention of shifting the ball wider than a couple of passes before smashing their way back into the All Blacks forwards. When the All Blacks did get the ball themselves, they did more or less the same thing. Both teams had each other in a clinch, and it looked like whoever could land a gut punch first would take the ultimate prize.

Both of them had the best view in the world of Donald's moment of glory. The kick sailed through just inside the right-hand upright and gave the All Blacks an ultimately unassailable lead. Not long after, Samuel was subbed for Ali Williams, but Owen stayed on the park alongside Woodcock. It remains the last time two All Blacks props have played the entirety of a test match.

It was worth the effort as the banged-up All Blacks won the game 8–7. It later turned out McCaw had played the entire tournament with a broken foot, but that didn't stop him riding in a ticker-tape parade through Auckland the next day.

That same year, Samuel and George's younger brother, Luke, had broken into the public consciousness as well. Their father Braeden, himself a former Manawatu rep and NZ Colt in the late '70s, had sent his sons south to Canterbury after they'd finished school to heighten their chances of rugby success. While it hadn't made him that popular in Palmerston North, the Whitelock patriarch's plan was working out perfectly. As well as two All Blacks, by 2011 Luke added to the honours by becoming the NZ Under-20s captain for their World Championship win in Italy.

Under coach Steve Hansen, the new world champions only got better over the next few seasons as they relentlessly built the side that would defend their title in 2015. Luke found himself part of those plans on the 2013 end-of-year tour to Japan and Europe, earning his first test cap in Tokyo. Like his brother, though, he was thwarted by another special All Black taking the spot he was after. It didn't help that Kieran Read then became captain of the team when McCaw retired after the next World Cup win.

In fact, it seemed like Luke was on course to join his brother

George as a one-test All Black. Meanwhile, Samuel had undergone the only real blip form-wise in his career the year before, getting replaced in the starting XV by Brodie Retallick against Argentina. He returned the next week against the Springboks and to date has never been dropped since. It was with Retallick that he found his number-one partner in the second row, as well.

Both Franks brothers went on to the Rugby World Cup in 2015, which proved to be a far less stressful experience for New Zealand. The All Blacks swept through the tournament and were seemingly only troubled once, although the scoreline in the 20–18 victory over the Springboks in their semi-final doesn't really tell the full story of the game. While it was admittedly a bit closer than they would have liked, the All Blacks had the game completely in control for the entire second half.

The final itself, against the Wallabies at Twickenham, was a complete walkover in contrast. Owen and Samuel got to start and had Dan Carter behind them, having perhaps the most perfect final game an All Black has ever played. Ben came on in the second half—a chance to make up for having to watch the last final on the sidelines of Eden Park. The final score: 34–17. Two World Cup final wins in a row.

It says an awful lot that a guy with one test's worth of experience was immediately promoted to captain, but that's exactly what happened to Luke when he was recalled.

It was Ben's last game for the All Blacks. He took up a contract in England, and left Owen to battle in the All Blacks scrum with

Samuel behind him. It wasn't until 2017 that Luke re-entered the picture, as the placeholder for the now vital Read.

It says an awful lot that a guy with one test's worth of experience was immediately promoted to captain, but that's exactly what happened to Luke when he was recalled. He led the side in a rare midweek fixture against a French XV in Lyon, then 11 days later found himself in the test side due to Read getting injured. This time he wasn't the captain, but the honour went to his brother Samuel—the first time two brothers had ever achieved that feat.

A year later, the All Blacks found themselves in Tokyo. By then, Luke had filled in for Read throughout the season and was in line for his seventh cap against Japan in a makeshift All Blacks side that was missing the top-line players, who had all already flown on for the next test in London. Steve Hansen held a press conference midweek, and gave a short, yet telling, reply when asked why he'd made Luke the captain.

'He's a Whitelock. They're born leaders.'

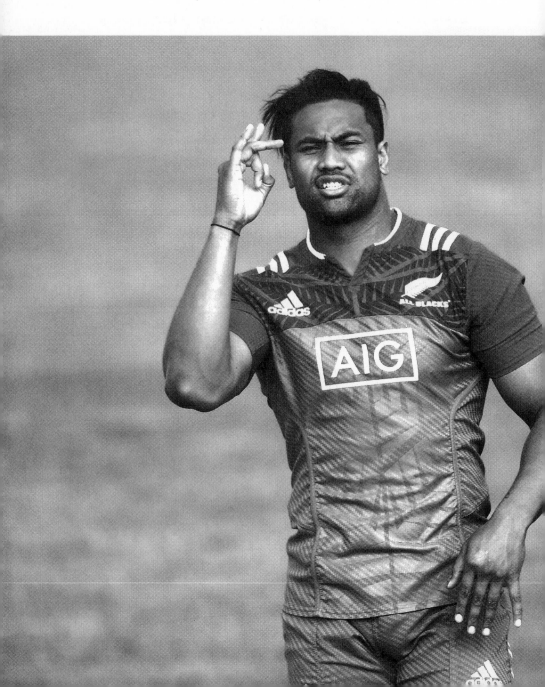

Julian (left) and Ardie Savea—two brothers whose careers have gone in different directions. **PHOTOSPORT**

JULIAN AND ARDIE SAVEA

THE SECOND-TO-LAST WEEK OF February 2019 is one that people are probably going to remember about Julian and Ardie Savea. One of them hit the headlines in a blaze of publicity, leading to a raft of conjecture on social media that effectively summed up his entire career so far. The other knuckled down and provided the literal driving force that got his team an unlikely victory.

Seven days of scrutiny. A time when both had the perceptions of themselves right there for the rugby world to see.

SATURDAY, 16 FEB 2019

The Hurricanes are facing the Waratahs at Brookvale Oval. In the days leading up to the game, the focus has been on the shocking state of the pitch—so bad it forced an NRL pre-season game to be moved to a different park. There are worries too about the Hurricanes side picked. Beauden Barrett is sitting out the game in the first of his World Cup-enforced stand-down periods, several players are on debut and the pack has a definite green edge to it after the loss of influential blindside Brad Shields the year before.

It's enough for a number of New Zealand pundits to write the team off, despite the fact that they still have a considerable number of All Blacks. The Hurricanes are typically a rusty side in round one, with their only convincing opening victory in the last few years coming against the lowly Sunwolves in Tokyo.

For a while, it looks like the critics might be right. Passes are dropped, set pieces butchered and needless penalties conceded. The only thing that appears to be going right is that the opposition seem too nervous to cash in on their good fortune. Compared to the fixture that preceded this one—a thrilling 24–22 win by the Crusaders over the Blues at Eden Park—the first half is a hard watch. At least the much-talked-about Brookvale Oval pitch is holding together.

If there's one thing you can say about Ardie, it's that he's a hard man to put down. Ever since he debuted for the Hurricanes in 2013, he's been all arms and legs whenever he gets the ball.

Not long before half-time, Ardie Savea decides he's going to do something about the rut the Hurricanes have found themselves in. If there's one thing you can say about Ardie, it's that he's a hard man to put down. Ever since he debuted for the Hurricanes in 2013, he's been all arms and legs whenever he gets the ball, twisting and turning his way through A-channels close to the ruck. Whenever he's in open space, his knees lift high and violently to deter anyone trying to go low and cut down his 100 kg frame.

The score is 9–3 to the Waratahs. The ball has been placed two metres out from their line by a Hurricanes forward pack that's finally got a bit of continuity going. Ardie waits, and intelligently spots the line that he'll attack just inside of the right-hand post. The padding around the post will impede the effectiveness of any Waratahs defender coming across from the right to try to hold him up. But first he needs to get across the line.

He puts his hands on the ball and scoops it up. His next move is to drive low and hard into the first defender, hooker Damien Fitzpatrick. He smashes into his midsection and Fitzpatrick is caught off-balance, even more so when Ardie wrenches his shoulders free of Damien's grasp and begins to turn his body anti-clockwise. Michael Hooper comes in to help, but it's too late—Ardie's momentum is sending him on a one-way trip to the ground, and there's no way the two Waratahs can stop him. The only man who can, number 8 Jack Dempsey, is on the other side of the padding, wondering what's just happened. Ardie lands heavily on top of the ball, scoring a try under the posts.

He almost gets another in the second half, in similar circumstances, but it's rubbed out by the TMO because of an infringement in the build-up. But it doesn't matter. This game is already going down as one of his landmark performances, win or lose. Ardie's work around the field has been outstanding. His tireless effort in an arm wrestle of a game is reminding everyone just why he's the current starting openside for the All Blacks, and that Sam Cane may well have a decent job on his hands to get the jersey back when he returns from a neck injury.

In the end, the Hurricanes scrape to a 20–19 win, albeit due to a shocking last-minute penalty miss by Waratahs first five Bernard Foley. They'll take it, is the general consensus at the end of the match. After all, it is going to be a long Super Rugby season that's started earlier than usual due to the impending World Cup at the year's end.

It's the first season that Ardie has been the only Savea in the Hurricanes. His brother Julian is playing out a cashed-up contract at glamour club Toulon in France. Given that the average New

Zealand rugby fan's knowledge and interest of the French Top 14 competition is minuscule, no one has paid much attention to the reports leaking through that Julian's time at the club hasn't exactly gone smoothly. You'd be hard-pressed to find anyone that could even name the team Toulon is playing that weekend.

SUNDAY, 17 FEB 2019

> The greater cause for the defeat was the Waratah pack's inability to turn up the dial physically when needed and inability, in particular, to cope with the terrific Ardie Savea. There was no mistaking the dominant back row force at Brookvale—it was the All Blacks No. 7.
>
> *—Sydney Morning Herald*

While Ardie is recovering from his mammoth performance against the Waratahs, Julian is getting ready to take the field on the other side of the world, where it's still Saturday. Toulon are due to meet Agen, a team placed near the bottom of the Top 14 competition. Toulon aren't faring much better, only one rung above them on the competition ladder in thirteenth place.

Barely anyone back home will have registered that Julian is playing at all, and even fewer would be able to explain what the permutations of winning or losing will mean to either side. While French rugby is a big talking point in Julian's homeland, it's only from the point of view of who will cash up and go over there as the next stage of their career. The fortunes of the teams they're going to are more or less unknown in the pubs and rugby clubs of Aotearoa. The only real news that makes the sports pages to do with the Top 14 is when a former All Black has an exceptionally good game, gets injured, or gets in trouble.

Julian Savea is about to do the latter, and everyone is going to know about it.

While French rugby is a big talking point in Julian's homeland, it's only from the point of view of who will cash up and go over there as the next stage of their career.

The game against Agen is, by French standards, about an average reflection of Top 14 play. Plenty of giant robotic forwards running into one another and kicking for territory. It's a competition where teams play to avoid losing, rather than to win. However, every now and then some actual rugby gets played that's worth watching.

Thirty-five minutes in, the Toulon forwards are smashed off their own ball in a ruck on Agen's 22. The ball is quickly spread wide to Jessy Jegerlehner, who shows good skills for a blindside flanker by stepping infield and brushing off a tackle, then kicking ahead along the deck for his winger Benito Masilevu to chase. Julian is back there, having dropped to cover after the turnover.

Julian is a former All Blacks winger, twice nominated for World Player of the Year. Benito Masilevu, despite having played test rugby for Fiji, is known more as a young Sevens prodigy from years before. He's been playing in France for the last five seasons, and is a year older than Julian.

At first, it looks like Jegerlehner's kick is too long to be anything more than a good way to pressure Julian to put the ball out close to his line. Agen would take that, but Masilevu has other ideas. Despite having a 10-metre handicap, he burns past Julian on the 22. As the ball rolls to the goal line, the former All Black makes a despairing dive for it, only to inadvertently knock it further away. All that Masilevu has to do is dive on the ball, and Julian gets a perfect view of his opponent's maiden try for Agen while he's sprawled out on the turf.

It's an important score. Agen go on to win the game 19–10, handing Toulon their tenth loss of the season. It's unclear exactly where Toulon owner Mourad Boudjellal has watched the game, but it is clear that the result has made him extremely upset. Putting this team together has cost him an absolute fortune and he doesn't seem to be the sort of person that likes getting let down by the people whose wages he pays.

All that Masilevu has to do is dive on the ball, and Julian gets a perfect view of his opponent's maiden try for Agen while he's sprawled out on the turf.

Boudjellal, who made his money in the comics-publishing business, is interviewed post-match by France's RMC Radio. When questioned about Julian's form, he says this: 'They must have swapped him on the plane [when he joined from Hurricanes]. If I were him I would apologise and go back to my home country.'

MONDAY, 18 FEB 2019

Back in New Zealand, rugby fans are waking up to the big story of the week.

Toulon president Mourad Boudjellal singled out ex-All Black Julian Savea following the club's latest defeat, saying he 'was no longer welcome'.

'I'm going to ask for a DNA test, this isn't the Savea that we signed. They must have changed him on the plane,' Boudjellal fumed on Sunday, the day after a 19–10 defeat to Agen.

The 2015 World Cup winner joined Toulon amid much fanfare last summer, but the 28-year-old has failed to replicate the form that saw him score 46 tries in 54 caps for New Zealand. With only two tries since signing for the Top 14 side Savea was no match for the speed of Fijian wing Benito Masilevu in Agen's second try.

—Fox Sports

TUESDAY, 19 FEB 2019

Boudjellal said next season would be difficult for the winger if he opts to come back for the second year of his deal.

'A one-year contract, he can do what he wants, it can be long for the club, a year, but especially very long for the player.

'For me, he is released.'

—TVNZ

By now the New Zealand press have had a full 24 hours to ruminate on Julian's performance and Boudjellal's histrionic response. It's not the first time the Toulon owner has come out swinging over the form of his players, nor even the first time he's publicly bagged some of his New Zealand imports.

In 2016, he criticised the form of Ma'a Nonu and Tom Taylor, along with former Wallaby Quade Cooper. While Cooper and Taylor exercised exit clauses in their contracts at the end of that season, Nonu saw his out before returning to New Zealand in late 2018. In 2012, Boudjellal was banned from attending games for 130 days for comparing the way Toulon was being refereed to anal porn. The man knows how to get attention, and it seems like this outburst against Julian is just another example in a string of trash talk by a man so far removed from New Zealand culture it's hard to know when to take him seriously.

But that's exactly what the media here do, running articles saying that he's been fired from Toulon and speculating on his next moves. Of course, he hasn't—leaving the club immediately would mean that Boudjellal would have to pay out his entire contract at once, which is rumoured to be over NZ$1.5 million a season.

'Take a minute to think about how your words can affect someone's life and their mental health,' Fatima Savea tweeted.

'And people wonder why mental health in rugby had become a big problem. Take a minute to be considerate of people's feelings instead of bashing them behind a keyboard or phone screen.'

She suggested Savea's form problems weren't all his own doing.

'With rugby you are only as good as your team. It's not an individual sport, it's a team sport and sometimes you can be let down by your team,' she said.

—Stuff

The press have gone to drink from their most trusted well when it comes to matters regarding Julian Savea—his wife, Fatima. The 24-year-old is never short of a word on social media regarding her husband's form, career decisions or even in-game analysis, so the current trend of simply churning out tweets and Instagram posts as news stories has made her the most famous All Black spouse of the decade. Any headline that involves Julian will invariably include Fatima at some point down the track, and this one is no different.

She is intensely loyal. It's admittedly admirable; who wouldn't want the support of their partner in their role? It's also a sign of the times. Social media has given the public the sort of insight into the mood of famous people that a newspaper never could, catching raw emotions that often get taken completely out of context. Both Julian and Fatima have grown up in a world where simply telling potentially thousands of your online followers how you feel is a natural, often several-times-a-day occurrence.

> **She's wise enough to choose her words carefully. She doesn't take aim at the man who has directly set out to belittle her husband in public, the man who is paying Julian's salary—rather, she targets the reaction to Boudjellal's words.**

'Outspoken' is usually prefixed to her name when it finds its way onto the pages of *Stuff* and the *New Zealand Herald*. It's 2019, though. Everyone who has a Twitter account is outspoken.

She's wise enough to choose her words carefully. She doesn't take aim at the man who has directly set out to belittle her husband in public, the man who is paying Julian's salary—rather, she targets the reaction to Boudjellal's words. Her Instagram page has been hit with disgruntled fan comments about Julian's form, so she takes to social media to show everyone the kind of messages the couple have been dealing with. Articles appear quickly on New Zealand online media sites, mostly made up of Fatima's posts.

WEDNESDAY, 20 FEB 2019

> There was a time when Julian Savea swept through tacklers with such ferocity that he was compared to the great Jonah Lomu. Within minutes of scoring three tries in the All Blacks' 62–13 win over France in the 2015 World Cup quarter-final in Cardiff, left wing Savea was hailed as one of the most ruthless ball runners on the planet. So it was inevitable his name would be mentioned in the same breath as the great Lomu, the deadly finisher who, sadly, was to die less than a month after the All Blacks won the Webb Ellis Cup at that tournament.
>
> *—Stuff*

Now that the facts of the situation have been established, the conversation has turned into what sort of player Julian Savea used to be, rather than the one he might be now. Of course, this is because hardly anyone in New Zealand knows what sort of player he is now—the only footage they've seen of Savea since he left the Hurricanes in 2018 is him getting left in the dust by Masilevu a few days earlier.

So we collectively cast our minds back to just how good he was when he broke into a post-World Cup-winning All Blacks side in 2012. It was a place he was destined to end up, after starring for the World Championship-winning New Zealand Under-20s team in 2010 and picking up the title of Under-20s Player of the Year. Big things were expected when he made his debut for Wellington and the Hurricanes in 2011, but his confidence and susceptibility under the high ball marred that season in Super Rugby and the Mitre 10 Cup. It seemed as though Julian might fade away into an age-grade trivia question, especially considering the Hurricanes environment wasn't exactly the most harmonious one when he was heading into his second season.

New coach and former All Blacks hooker Mark Hammett had decided to gut the team of what he felt was a degenerative culture among the senior players. Out went Ma'a Nonu, Andrew Hore and Piri Weepu, and in came a massive spotlight of media attention on whether Hammett had made the right call. For a while in 2012, it actually looked like he had.

> **New coach and former All Blacks hooker Mark Hammett had decided to gut the team of what he felt was a degenerative culture among the senior players.**

Julian enjoyed a breakout season, scoring nine tries and generally living up to the hype that had him labelled as the next Jonah Lomu when he was an age-grade star. However, he was overshadowed by another member of the Hurricanes back three. Andre Taylor was almost a complete opposite type of winger to Julian, small, slight and agile. He had such a prolific season that it was his name that was being bandied about more often as the impending test series with Ireland was looming.

New All Blacks coach Steve Hansen liked what he saw of Julian, though. He viewed the Hurricanes winger as the strike option on one side of the field, complemented by the tall Israel Dagg at fullback and Zac Guildford on the other wing. Julian was named in the starting line-up for the first test against Ireland. Also making their debuts at Eden Park that night were a young halfback from the Highlanders, Aaron Smith, and impressive Chiefs lock Brodie Retallick.

By the end of the game, everyone in the rugby world knew who Julian Savea was. The 21-year-old had blasted his way onto the test scene, scoring three tries in the All Blacks' 42–10 hiding of Ireland. Maybe he was the second coming of Lomu, after all; the hapless Irish were the first to really feel the full force of Lomu's power back in 1995.

By the end of the game, everyone in the rugby world knew who Julian Savea was. The 21-year-old had blasted his way onto the test scene

After his phenomenal debut, Julian went on to score nine more test tries in 2012. Then eight more in 2013, a year in which the All Blacks won every single test they played. Then, 11 more in 2014.

Back in those heady days, Julian was one of the biggest names in the sport, acquiring the nickname of 'The Bus'. This upcoming weekend, though, he won't even be in the squad for Toulon's next Top 14 game.

Hurricanes coach John Plumtree has opted to rest his star number seven Ardie Savea for this weekend's Super Rugby clash.

'Ardie has got a long season in place so I gave him the week off. These are the decisions that are really tough for me and the team 'cause Ardie is obviously a star player. But again it's an opportunity for Du'Plessis Kirifi and Sam Henwood to show me what they are capable of against the great loose forwards at the Crusaders.'

—TVNZ

It's team-naming day for the next round of Super Rugby. Despite being the difference between winning and losing the weekend before against the Waratahs, Ardie Savea is in the same position as his brother—but for different reasons. His resting is, despite Plumtree's seemingly magnanimous verbal gesture, an enforced break because of his importance to the upcoming All Blacks campaign of the year. Just a few months prior, Ardie cemented his spot as an integral part of the World Cup defence in Japan after taking over the openside flanker role from Sam Cane.

Before that, though, his career had followed a similar path to Julian's. The boys grew up in Miramar, in Wellington's eastern suburbs. It's an area dotted with state houses that's been feeling the effects of creeping gentrification for a while now. Nonetheless, the local all-boys high school Rongotai College is seen as the poorer younger brother of the more affluent Wellington College across town, the latter typically dominating the achievement standings due to its huge enrolment catchment.

Rongotai have punched above their weight in the Premier One College Division for the school's entire history. They're regarded as historically one of the top four rugby schools in the city, and won the competition in 2003, although (just like the rich folk starting to take over the real estate in the area) nearby private school Scots College has muscled its way into the top ranks.

By the time the Savea brothers made it to Rongotai, which is located on the windswept tip of land hugging the airport, the school could already boast of producing one of the most prolific All Blacks of recent history. Ma'a Nonu remains a local legend, and back then he was constantly selected in the national side, forming the midfield combination with Conrad Smith.

Julian and Ardie followed in his footsteps to make the Rongotai first XV. While Julian naturally spent his time creating havoc on the wing, Ardie played on the openside flank. However, his sublime ball skills and pace meant that by the time he reached his senior year, Ardie had been moved to centre. The brothers' talents couldn't help the school win another title, but it was enough to get them both on the national selection radar.

Before he left Rongotai, Ardie was given the honour of being head boy, and his presence on the school-hall podium was one that demanded respect. By then he had grown into an almost 100 kg unit. When he got up to speak, it wasn't uncommon for the student body to stomp and clap 'We Will Rock You', knowing that Ardie would probably admonish them for bad behaviour on the after-school buses.

Ardie made the New Zealand Under-20s team, just like Julian. He debuted for Wellington aged only 18 in 2012, the same year his brother embarked on his prolific first season in the All Blacks.

Astute Wellington rugby followers, especially those who'd kept an eye on Ardie's progression at Rongotai, were breathlessly claiming that it was just a matter of time before the brothers would appear alongside one another in a black jersey.

They were right, but Ardie's introduction to the All Blacks wasn't as explosive as Julian's. After forcing his way into Hammett's Hurricanes squad the following year, Ardie was picked by Steve Hansen as an All Blacks 'apprentice' on the end-of-year tour to Japan and Europe. It completely took the intrigue over his selection out of the picture, but it meant that he could confidently look forward to making his debut at some stage. However, it soon became clear that Hansen was grooming Ardie to slot into the loose forward depth chart after the 2015 World Cup, and that Ardie would have to wait out Richie McCaw's swansong.

FRIDAY, 22 FEB 2019

En tant que joueur, je sais comment je réagirais si on me piquait comme ça. Mais chacun réagit comme il veut. Certains diront que c'est violent, d'autres que ça ne leur fait ni chaud ni froid ou encore que ça fait du bien. Julian est un faux problème, c'est collectivement que nous avons failli.

As a player, I know how I would react if I was stung like that. But everyone reacts as he wants. Some will say that it is harsh, others that it does not make a difference or that it feels good. But Julian is a false problem, collectively we have failed as a group.

—Toulon coach Patrice Collazo, Rugbyrama Eurosport

While it's Friday in New Zealand, Thursday evening in France is also team-naming time. Julian's axing from the team has made headlines in Europe, but it comes with a distinct asterisk of support from his coach. Patrice Collazo, the burly cauliflower-eared former prop who played in France's top flight for 15 seasons, knows full well the pressure that his winger is under because he's been under it himself since being named Toulon coach the previous June. He is making it clear that while Julian hasn't exactly set the world on fire in his time in the Top 14, no one else at Toulon has either. Just now, he has bigger issues than Boudjellal shooting his mouth off.

In the same interview, his words turn into what could be translated as a warning, though. 'When I talk about the club to a player, I have to see something on his face, his eyes. If I do not have that, it is an end. The hardest part is when you talk about the club and there is no reaction . . . There is a duty to perpetuate something compared to those who have gone before.'

He had the almost unprecedented honour of having the normally staid New Zealand crowd chant his name.

Already during the week there's been talk that the real motivation behind Boudjellal's outburst was pent-up anger at Julian for taking a month out of his season over Christmas to go home and attend Ardie's wedding. The year before had seen the brothers' careers diverting for the first time—they'd played for the same school, club, province and Super Rugby team, and finally together in the All Blacks. But in 2018 Julian's path had taken him to the other side of the world, while Ardie had entrenched himself firmly into the All Blacks.

Two years previously, though, Ardie had made his test debut against Wales at Eden Park, then scored a try in his second test—in his home town of Wellington. He had the almost unprecedented honour of having the normally staid New Zealand crowd chant his name. It had been a big year in the capital, with the Hurricanes finally managing to break their 20-year-long wait for a Super Rugby title. While Ardie had been front and centre of the thrilling campaign, the business end marked the tipping point in the decline in Julian's fortunes. New coach Chris Boyd, who had taken over from Hammett, unceremoniously dumped Julian to the bench for the finals and replaced him with Jason Woodward.

By the end of that year, it was hard to gauge the future for the Savea brothers—and few would have predicted the scenario that was to play out.

Nevertheless, Julian was selected for the All Blacks by Hansen, and started on the wing against Wales. It meant that Julian and Ardie became the forty-fourth set of brothers to play for the All Blacks. And while Julian missed the next test, he ended up starting nine out of the 10 tests he was picked for that year. Ardie, meanwhile, was facing a battle with Sam Cane and Matt Todd for the spot left by McCaw, and Cane had a distinct advantage given that he'd been made captain for the one World Cup game McCaw missed. Ten out of Ardie's 12 games in 2016 were ones in which he came off the bench. By the end of that year, it was hard to gauge the future for the Savea brothers—and few would have predicted the scenario that was to play out in February 2019.

After their close shave against the Waratahs, the Hurricanes are exposed against the champion Crusaders in Christchurch in round two of Super Rugby. Plumtree's willingness, indeed happiness, to rest Ardie was either a blatant lie or some decidedly wishful thinking on his part. The forward pack barely fires a shot in the first hour of the game, and the lack of go-forward that Ardie brought to Brookvale the week before is evident.

Let's just say Hurricanes fans who couldn't catch the game live and were forced to record the match, won't be rushing for a seat in front of their televisions to flick it on when they're freed up.

No, this was one which will swiftly be banished from their recording devices. No doubt the Hurricanes coaching staff will be quick to flush it, too.

To be blunt, their first half performance was the stuff nightmares are made of, and they could quite easily have trailed by more than 24–0.

Sure, they were missing key players such as Beauden Barrett, Ardie Savea and Vaea Fifita, but it's not as if Codie Taylor, Sam Whitelock and Kieran Read fronted for their opposition.

—Stuff

Worse still, the main antagonist in the loss is Matt Todd, Ardie's current nemesis for an All Blacks spot. Right now, he can't afford to concede any ground to Todd, a player so highly rated by Hansen that the coach convinced New Zealand Rugby to bend their eligibility rules and allow him to play on the 2018 end-of-year tour (Todd had been away on a short-term contract in Japan).

Since Cane's serious injury in October 2018, picked up halfway through a test against the Springboks in Pretoria, Ardie has been entrusted with the starting openside flanker's jersey. That game in Pretoria capped what had been a remarkable change in fortune for Ardie, who started the year with serious question marks over his size and effectiveness at the breakdown in test rugby. He scored the winning try in the thrilling win over the Boks, as well as blitzing criticism by having a stint at number 8. He went on to start every test on the end-of-year tour.

Nothing and no one stands still in rugby, though, and he knows he'll have to fight to maintain his position in 2019.

He scored the winning try in the thrilling win over the Boks, as well as blitzing criticism by having a stint at number 8. He went on to start every test on the end-of-year tour.

Julian's 2018 was, of course, markedly different from his brother's. He had found himself increasingly out of favour in 2017, as the Hurricanes battled to defend their Super Rugby title. While his side did better than the perennially struggling Blues, the Auckland team had unearthed Rieko Ioane, the man who would soon be earmarked for the gap that a struggling Julian would leave in the All Blacks.

By the time the first test against the British & Irish Lions at Eden Park rolled around in June 2017, Rieko had done exactly that. Faster, taller and (most importantly) younger, he almost replicated Julian's debut with two tries in the 30–15 win. No one was really that surprised. After all, Julian had reached his shelf life as an All Blacks winger: 27 years old, 40-odd tries.

In fact, it's almost scary how similar the end of Savea's career is to other prolific All Blacks try-scorers. At one point it seemed as though it was just a matter of time before he'd smash Doug Howlett's record of 49 test tries, but his 46th against Manu Samoa would be his last. That ranked him second on the all-time list, alongside Christian Cullen and Joe Rokocoko. Only two behind them is Jeff Wilson, then comes Jonah Lomu. All of them ended their All Blacks careers at around the age of 27, which Julian had turned in 2017.

It was inevitable that halfway through 2018, Julian would sign with an overseas club. He saw out the Mitre 10 Cup with Wellington and moved to France to play for Toulon. At the time, he would have been seen as a star signing but, right now, things are looking rocky.

It was inevitable that halfway through 2018, Julian would sign with an overseas club. He saw out the Mitre 10 Cup with Wellington and moved to France to play for Toulon.

As the week in rugby draws to a close, amid the death throes of the Julian Savea saga, there's an unnecessary addendum on social media: Boudjellal's daughter posts a sarcastic tweet because the game he's been dropped for results in a good win for Toulon. Fatima responds with a thinly veiled reminder of manners on Instagram. But that's the world Julian lives in now. The media hover over every move he makes, regardless of what's happening on the field. One upside is that at least now New Zealand fans are a little bit more clued up about what's going on in the Top 14.

Ardie's Hurricanes prepare for their next challenge, against the Brumbies the following Friday night. He's expected to come straight back into the starting XV. Like Plumtree said, though, 2019 will be a long season for Ardie Savea.

Just what the season will bring for Julian is anyone's guess.

A MERE THREE MONTHS LATER, Ardie has played around 800 minutes for the Hurricanes as they lock down a Super Rugby play-off spot. That's an average of 78.5 minutes per game—apparently well over his quota according to the All Blacks regulations set down at the start of the season. Over in France, it turns out Boudjellal was full of hot air. Julian declares he's staying on at Toulon, to play out his now-confirmed $1.65-million-a-season contract.

Another trophy locked away: Beauden (left) and Scott Barrett carry the Bledisloe Cup around the field in 2017. Along with younger sibling Jordie, the Barretts encapsulate the spirit of the All Blacks brothers who have come before them.
PHOTOSPORT/DEREK MORRISON

BEAUDEN, SCOTT AND JORDIE BARRETT

IT MAKES SENSE TO END with the Barretts. Beauden, Scott and Jordie encapsulate almost all of the aspects of all the brothers that have come before them—they are, in effect, the ultimate set for the modern age of All Blacks rugby.

They have a creation myth, like the one the Warbricks handed on to the All Blacks story. It's hard to go past any piece of punditry about the Taranaki family that doesn't mention how their dad Kevin 'Smiley' Barrett played flanker for the Hurricanes in the first years of Super Rugby, and about how he announced once he retired that he was 'off to make some All Blacks'. Like all myths, while it sounds good, it isn't true. By the time Smiley had played his last game for the Hurricanes, a semi-final loss to the Brumbies in Canberra to conclude their stunning 1997 season, all of his future All Blacks sons had already been born.

By then, Beauden was six years old, Scott four, and Jordie three months old. His eldest son Kane would also go on to a professional rugby career, and Smiley and mother Robyn would add Blake, Zara, Ella and Jenna in the next few years.

Like the Brookes, there is an outdoors component that helped grow their talent. The Barrett family shifted to Meath in Ireland in 2000, where Smiley worked as a farm manager and the oldest boys played Gaelic football. You don't need to be an expert on the sport to know that some of its key skill sets are more than useful when transferred to rugby, and that's exactly what they did when they returned to New Zealand after a year and a half.

Like the Meads, one of the brothers is far more prominent than the others. Beauden, the human highlight reel of a first five, has widely been regarded as the best player in the world for most of his career. In fact, he's been officially bestowed with that honour twice. Beauden Barrett's name is now in the realms of superstar status, and every career move he makes is closely followed by a media pack that ran cringeworthy live updates of his January 2019 wedding.

But, like the Clarkes, the brother in the engine room is a complete contrast to the flashy skills of the other two. Scott has developed as an outstanding lock, grafting away to provide the ball supply that his brothers can turn into tries.

Beauden, the human highlight reel of a first five, has widely been regarded as the best player in the world for most of his career.

Like the Whettons, they hold a unique record in terms of brotherhood as the only three brothers to have played in a test match together. Also, like AJ, one of them spent a frustrating period at the start of his career waiting for an opportunity to make a starting place his own. When Beauden did, he grabbed it with both hands and became the pre-eminent player in his position.

Like the Bachops, there is the fact that one of them will spend his time playing against, rather than alongside, the other two. Scott is now a mainstay with the Crusaders, a team that few leave for another opportunity in New Zealand. Beauden and Jordie have established themselves as integral parts of the team their dad played for, the Hurricanes. Every year, we get the Barrett Bowl when Beauden and Jordie face Scott in what's become the biggest rivalry for either side in their Super Rugby.

Like the Saveas, there will be massive conjecture as to where their post-All Blacks careers will take them. Already, Beauden is being lined up to be farmed out for a year in Japan so that the All Blacks can retain his services while having someone else pay the wages that he's probably worth. Exactly where Jordie finds himself after the World Cup in 2019 may well be part of the ongoing saga of offshore player drain and of what happens to the All Blacks if they decide to go or stay.

Beauden was the first of the brothers to make the All Blacks, but if you were to make a prediction as to how his career was going to pan out halfway through 2015, it seemed like he was on course to become the most prolific bench player of all time: 33 out of his first 39 appearances for the All Blacks since his debut against Ireland in 2012. He'd had a few starts in 2014, one of which was an epic loss to the Springboks at Ellis Park. By now, Dan Carter had returned to be the starting first five, though he was beginning to come under immense pressure from Aaron Cruden. Beauden's utility value was a blessing and a curse—it meant that he probably wouldn't get a starting shot at either first five or fullback, because he was more useful on the bench as cover for both.

Even the fact that his attacking flair was on show when he'd be injected into the game seemed to be evidence that he was better suited to come in and finish a game off, rather than be trusted to run the backline from kick-off. His first test start came at fullback anyway, and the general consensus was that it was there that he would be most useful. Which is why, by the time the World Cup year came around, his name barely featured in what would become the prime debate of the season.

A lot of folks like to give the *New Zealand Herald*'s sports columnist Chris Rattue an inordinate amount of grief for his bold and ultimately highly inaccurate prediction that Carter ought to have been dropped for the World Cup campaign. It's unfair, given that at the time, Rattue and quite a lot of others were working off the basis that Cruden would be the one to take over. That wasn't such a stretch at the time—Cruden had recently won two Super Rugby titles with the Chiefs and was in hot form. Also, by then Carter was 33.

Unfortunately for Rattue and everyone else in that camp, Cruden broke his leg in the lead-up to the tournament. If he'd stayed fit and started, this story may well have been very different.

Instead Carter played, found some of the form that made him the best player in the world for a good chunk of the last decade, and then played a superb game in the final at Twickenham. The moment belonged to him, scoring 19 points including a long-range dropped goal in the 34–17 win over the Wallabies. But, in a portent of things to come, Beauden came onto the field and scored the last try—chasing down a kick ahead by Ben Smith to outgun the tired defenders and sealing the win. But it didn't just do that—his performances across the tournament, including getting a start at first five against Namibia, effectively cleared the slate for the next year's battle for the starting spot with Cruden.

It also helped that in 2016 his Hurricanes side finally broke through and won a Super Rugby title, after 20 seasons of trying. Beauden was a leading hand in what ended up being the most thrilling regular-season finish in the tournament's history, with the Hurricanes leaping from fifth to first on the table with a 35–10 win over Scott's Crusaders side, even scoring a cheeky try to finish the game. He got another a few weeks later in the final against the Lions at a frozen Westpac Stadium in Wellington—the maiden championship victory ironically coming off the back of denying every team they played in the finals a try and a downright arm wrestle in the decider. It was a far cry from the image the team had carved out for themselves over their history, especially the season that had seen them score 544 points. Beauden had top-scored with 223 of those.

> **While Cruden's injury that kept him out of the World Cup had left the door ajar for Beauden, the next test would see it well and truly kicked down.**

One of the games they'd dropped in the course of the season was a 28–27 result to Cruden's Chiefs. Steve Hansen went with Cruden for the first two tests of the year against Wales. The first was a scratchy 39–21 win at Eden Park, which the Welsh had even led at half-time. While Cruden's injury that kept him out of the World Cup had left the door ajar for Beauden, the next test would see it well and truly kicked down. Unfortunately for Cruden, who had battled cancer as a teenager to make it to being an All Black, the key moment came when he was injured after half an hour of the second test in Wellington. Beauden entered the fray, set up Ben Smith for a try, then scored one himself in front of the same crowd that had cheered him on to Super Rugby glory. Final score 36–22.

He started the next test in Dunedin, and scored 26 against

Wales, which was slaughtered 46–6. Then the next, where the Wallabies were pounded 42–8. Then the next six, in which the All Blacks outscored their opponents 257–86. Beauden Barrett could do no wrong, and even had a Facebook page started in his honour called 'Beaudenism'. It sat under the category of 'religious organisation'.

There have been plenty of rumours and speculation about the circumstances surrounding the next game Beauden started, though. One thing is for sure: it was the first game in which two of the Barrett brothers would feature. Scott had impressed Steve Hansen enough that he was included on the end-of-year tour, and the All Blacks travelled to Chicago for the first of their two matches against Ireland.

Out of all the weeks you'd want to be in Chicago, this was it. But maybe not if you were planning on playing a rugby test against Ireland at the end of it. The Cubs had famously won baseball's World Series, for the first time in 108 years, and to say that the people of Chicago were pleased is perhaps the biggest understatement in the history of sports. Official estimates put the number of people that showed up to the victory parade at five million, which is a little hard to believe since that's twice the city's population and would make it potentially the largest gathering in human history, but the density of the celebration led media outlets to breathlessly report it as the truth. Whatever the number, it was a week of partying and celebration, and the All Blacks were at ground zero.

It's hard not to think that it affected the way they played, at a packed-out Soldier Field. After all, this was a gimmick game for their sponsor AIG to show off their new toy set, the best team in the world at any sport, ever. At the same time, it's pretty hard to try and make excuses for the All Blacks because they'd never do it themselves. But things looked mighty ominous when they walked out and found themselves in front of a 62,000-strong crowd mostly wearing green.

To make things even more tricky, Scott found himself on the bench behind an out-of-position Jerome Kaino and fellow rookie Patrick Tuipulotu. Those selections hadn't escaped the attention of Ireland coach Joe Schmidt, or his team. By the time Scott made his debut as an All Black in the forty-fifth minute, they were on the wrong end of a 25–8 deficit, which became 30–8 only a couple of minutes later.

But things looked mighty ominous when they walked out and found themselves in front of a 62,000-strong crowd mostly wearing green.

It was the complete opposite of when his brother had come off the bench to debut four years earlier against the Irish in Hamilton. That night, Beauden strolled onto the field with his team up 26–0, which eventuated into a record 60–0 hiding. That's definitely another reason the Irish were so desperate to win—in over a century they'd never beaten the All Blacks, and more often than not they'd been humiliated trying.

There's been so much talk about the Irish effort in the Chicago game in the years since that one aspect is often overlooked: the All Blacks came back to be within one score of getting the lead back. Scott's debut ended up being an outstanding game and he scored a fantastic try, running off a short ball by Liam Squire and then smartly stretching out to plant the ball over his head. It made the score 30–29 and, with 15 minutes to go, it seemed like the All Blacks were going to run away with a high-scoring but tactically dreadful victory.

Except the Irish knew this story all too well. There was no point sitting back and trying to defend their way out of this, so they absorbed the gut punch and got back to their feet. In a stunning last 10 minutes, they smashed the All Blacks right in the mouth, scoring a penalty and another try to seal a 40–29 win. Beauden's debut had been a historic win over Ireland. Scott's was now a historic loss.

The All Blacks got their revenge a fortnight later, in Dublin. Such was the intensity of the backlash and restoration of mana, the Irish media, who had (rightfully) crowed long and loud about the magnitude of the breaking of their 111-year duck against the All Blacks, suddenly turned into a hysterical mob. They claimed that the All Blacks had deliberately gone out to hurt their team in the 21–9 win, in which Beauden was awarded man of the match. They weren't wrong, but the reaction suggested more than a few of them had never seen a game of rugby before.

While this was going on, Jordie had been playing for Canterbury in the Mitre 10 Cup. Despite the boys having grown up in Taranaki and attending Francis Douglas Memorial College, Scott had originally followed the path of success that the Whitelock brothers, Kieran Read, Richie McCaw and so many others had taken by heading to Christchurch to maximise his rugby potential. By the time Jordie left school, following his brother south seemed like the smartest option, and he enjoyed a provincial title win with Canterbury in his first season.

The brilliance of Beauden, and the hard-working potential of

Scott, meant that Jordie's pedigree was seemingly unquestionable. A fight for his services erupted between the Crusaders and Hurricanes, and ultimately it was the team of his father and brother that won. Jordie therefore holds an unusual place in modern rugby, as maybe the only young, talented player the Crusaders have gone after that they haven't got.

He debuted for the Hurricanes the next season as the fullback behind Beauden. The defending champion team's form was even better than the year before, leading the competition with 96 tries. Jordie bagged seven of them, but the team couldn't repeat its heroics of the previous year, as the Lions got their revenge in a semi-final in Johannesburg. Beauden and Jordie got to watch on as Scott's Crusaders went to Ellis Park the next week and won the final.

Jordie therefore holds an unusual place in modern rugby, as maybe the only young, talented player the Crusaders have gone after that they haven't got.

By then, the much-hyped British & Irish Lions tour was just around the corner. It had been 12 years since they'd last come to New Zealand, and the general consensus was that they would receive another hiding like they had in 2005.

The confidence of the New Zealand fans was somewhat misplaced—after all, the Lions did contain a healthy contingent of Irishmen who had beaten the All Blacks just eight months previously. But it didn't help that it took them a good couple of weeks to stop playing like they'd just been introduced to one another five minutes before kick-off.

At the same time, the All Blacks had hastily arranged a warm-up game at Eden Park against Manu Samoa. It wasn't only the eventual 78–0 that showed the massive disparity between the teams, as a good number of the Samoans took the field in jerseys that clearly didn't fit. The test was also Jordie's first, like his brothers coming off the bench to make an impact straight away. All of the precocious talent he possessed was summed up with his first touch of the ball; after catching a high kick he immediately threw a behind-the-back flick pass infield. He was, however, part of the ever-crowded back three mix for the All Blacks—he would need to find a way past one of Ben Smith, Israel Dagg and Waisake Naholo, as well as the newly capped Rieko Ioane.

The test series began in earnest at Eden Park, but the first match ended the way most had expected. Ioane scored two tries in the comfortable 30–15 win, and the series moved to Wellington where it was presumed the All Blacks would simply repeat the process and consign the 2017 Lions to the dustbin of rugby history. It certainly appeared that would be the case as the midweek side blew a healthy lead to draw 31-all with the Hurricanes, in a game where Jordie did his selection case no harm at all with a dominant display. He may well have been thinking he'd be in line for a call-up in the third test—after all, the All Blacks had thought nothing of ringing the changes in the final test of the 2005 series to send a not-so-subtle message to the UK about what they thought of the supposed best of their talent.

But 25 minutes into the second test, with the scores locked at 3–3, everything changed. Sonny Bill Williams drove his shoulder into the face of Anthony Watson, leaving referee Jérôme Garcès with no option but to send him off. Never give a sucker a chance, because the Lions grabbed it and started playing like the team that thousands of fans from the home unions had travelled halfway around the world to see.

The bowl-shaped Westpac Stadium in Wellington is often maligned for having the seats too far away from the action, and for lacking in atmosphere. That probably says more about the painfully conservative nature of New Zealand rugby fans, because when it was half-full with red-clad Lions supporters who knew their team was in with a sniff of pulling off an upset, the place turned into a molten cauldron of will and desire. If a jumbo jet had flown over the top when Toby Faletau scored the Lions' first try, no one would have heard it. If one had crashed nearby when Conor Murray scored their second, whoever survived wasn't getting any help from anyone screaming their lungs out at the rugby.

Never give a sucker a chance, because the Lions grabbed it and started playing like the team that thousands of fans from the home unions had travelled halfway around the world to see.

The Irish halfback, who had played such a huge role in the Chicago upset, had made the score 21-all. Despite being down a man, the All Blacks had readjusted their game plan and relied on Beauden's boot to win them the test, and up until 10 minutes to go it looked like it was going to work. He'd kicked seven penalties, and if they'd pulled it off he would have been hailed as a hero. However, with four minutes to go, an extremely debatable penalty against prop Charlie Faumuina for tackling his opposite

Kyle Sinckler in the air gave the Lions a shot from straight out in front. Owen Farrell slammed it home to make it 24–21, and that was the end of an epic test match. The series, so widely predicted to be a whitewash that most of the British journalists who had travelled with the team had to hurriedly make accommodation arrangements for a week they originally thought would offer only a dead rubber match, was headed for a decider with the sort of intensity reserved for a World Cup final.

Of course, after any All Blacks loss comes the post-mortem, and with it the focus on the fact that never mind the seven shots Beauden had got, he'd also missed several. This is where the first real voices of heresy in the cult of Beaudenism appeared, and they haven't gone anywhere since.

> **Of course, after any All Blacks loss comes the post-mortem, and with it the focus on the fact that never mind the seven shots Beauden had got, he'd also missed several.**

Jordie got his call-up in the third test back at Eden Park, due to injuries to Naholo and Ioane. It marked the first time three brothers had ever played in the same test for the All Blacks, with Beauden starting and Scott coming off the bench. He started at fullback and, like the rest of the All Blacks, was watching on in horror after 12 minutes as the Lions looked like they would score out wide. Beauden came out of nowhere to grab an intercept and swing play 90 metres downfield, and then regrouped to put in a cross-kick for his brother to bat down and set up debutant Ngani Laumape for the opening try.

After 35 minutes, the roles were reversed as Laumape threw a brilliant offload to set up Jordie for a try in the corner. Beauden's conversion, crucially, sailed wide. Like the second test, though, the third would be remembered for a moment of refereeing. It's inaccurate to call it a decision, because Romain Poite's actions with the scores locked at 15-all was more of a conference call. He'd originally pinged Lions hooker Ken Owens for playing the ball in an offside position off a kick-off with three minutes to go. However, in an unprecedented move, he conferred with his assistant Garcès in French and turned off his mic so no one could hear what they said. When he walked back to the mark, he awarded the All Blacks a scrum instead.

At least 999 times out of 1000, the penalty would have stood. Beauden would have had a chance from about 43 metres out on an angle to the right of the posts to snatch a dramatic victory in what had turned into a pulsating test. Had he done so, it's unlikely that much protestation about his goal kicking under pressure would have been heard ever since. But he didn't, because it was the one time in the history of rugby that a ref decided to change his mind. The game and series were drawn, and the entire stadium felt like a party where the cops had shown up and told everyone to go home.

After the return to health of Naholo and Ioane, and despite his impressive test in the decider that ended up not being a decider, Jordie wasn't required for the rest of the year's test schedule. Beauden and Scott played in one record 57–0 hiding of the Springboks in Albany, then one absolute classic in Cape Town where the dormant rivalry between the two sides was shocked back to life with a 25–24 thriller. Beauden was given the captaincy for a game against the Barbarians at Twickenham on the end-of-year tour that served more as a thinly veiled All Blacks trial.

New Zealand Rugby had contrived to stack the Barbarians with mostly fringe New Zealand players, including promising Canterbury and Crusaders first five Richie Mo'unga. After that game, he joined the All Blacks squad—and the talk around just who should be wearing the number 10 jersey for test matches. Also in the picture was Damian McKenzie, who had been Cruden's replacement at the Chiefs.

By the end of the 2018 Super Rugby season, that talk had become a serious debate between the merits of all three. Mo'unga had a stunning campaign as the Crusaders retained their championship from the year before. It didn't help Beauden that the Hurricanes exited the competition in the semi-finals in a loss to Mo'unga's team, with many viewing it as an exclusive one-on-one showdown for the first-five position. McKenzie had been the standout in a Chiefs side banged up with injuries, and somewhat surprisingly he got a start in the last test against a woeful French side that toured in June, with Beauden rested.

Whatever doubt there was over Beauden's form should have been firmly put to rest as the All Blacks destroyed the Wallabies over the course of a week in August, though. He scored one try in the 38–13 win in Sydney, and then the next weekend he notched up a stunning four tries in the 40–12 result.

But it only silenced the chatter for a couple of weeks. The next test, in Wellington against the Springboks, was to be another lightning rod for critics of Beauden—and now Jordie as well. Even though it all started so well.

After five minutes, Beauden set Jordie up for a slick try. Then Aaron Smith scored to make it a comfortable lead and it looked like the All Blacks were going to dish out the same sort of hiding they'd given to the Wallabies. But then, after 25 minutes, Jordie's impetuousness got the better of him, and he threw a quick lineout infield that took a wicked bounce in front of Ben Smith before popping into the hands of Willie le Roux, who scored next to the posts. He wasn't alone; Anton Lienart-Brown tossed an intercept for Cheslin Kolbe to scoot away and score from as well.

While that criticism was warranted— it's perfectly reasonable to single out missed conversions as game-changing moments—what happened in the dying stages of the game was a little bit different.

The All Blacks were more than staying in touch; in fact, they ended up scoring six tries to the Springboks' five in a high-octane test match. The problem was that Beauden was having possibly the worst night of his entire life with the boot, failing to convert Jordie, Codie Taylor and Ardie Savea's tries—with the last two being in positions that you'd expect a primary-school-grade rep player to make without even blinking. His opposite, Handré Pollard, had kicked four conversions and a penalty.

But while that criticism was warranted—it's perfectly reasonable to single out missed conversions as game-changing moments—what happened in the dying stages of the game was a little bit different. The All Blacks, down by 36–34 and in possession in the Springbok 22, pressed hard to find a winner. Their game plan was working perfectly, too. By smashing away at the line toward the left-hand side of the posts, they'd opened up a huge overlap on the right, where McKenzie and Ben Smith stood waiting to run in the winning try. Only winger Aphiwe

Dyantyi, who had already scored two tries, was marking them.

Dyantyi knew it was now or never. The ball came from the ruck and, summoning every last energy reserve, he sprinted up and dived at McKenzie, who had hesitated at the winger's stunning speed off the mark. Dyantyi made a play at McKenzie's arm, knocked the ball loose, and the game was over. One year earlier, the Springboks had conceded 57 points against the All Blacks; now they'd had two stunning finishes in a row and won the latest edition of the grandest rivalry in rugby.

The talk afterward, while paying tribute to the Springboks, was focused on why Beauden hadn't taken a dropped goal. After all, they were only metres away from the goalposts. Those critics, though, neglected to note that he'd never once landed a dropped goal in his career. Plus, despite putting on a substandard performance for much of the test, the plan at the end was sound. Going for a winning try when they were within penalty or dropped-goal deficit had worked the year before against the Wallabies in Dunedin, in which Beauden himself had scored under the posts for a 35–29 win. So it was well within the realms of logic that the All Blacks would go for a play that they had practised, as opposed to handing the ball to a player who hadn't kicked a dropped goal before.

But the notion that he hadn't stepped up and taken the opportunity stuck with Beauden. He'd make sure by the end of the year that everyone would know he could drop a goal if his team needed to.

The fallout also affected Jordie. Seen as a liability after his rush of blood that led to the Boks' try, he slipped down the depth chart and only really just made it onto the end-of-year tour to Japan and the UK. He was given a chance to start in the test against

Japan alongside a host of new faces in Steve Hansen's expanded squad, only to see his first kick in play charged down and result in a Japanese try. It didn't have quite the same consequences as his last blooper, as the All Blacks eventually ran out winners 69–31.

Beauden, Scott and the rest of the All Blacks had already touched down in London for what had, a year before, been billed as the heavyweight clash between the two top sides in the world. Since then, though, England's fortunes had gone from a side that had won a record 18 tests in a row to dropping five in the past season. The focus was more on the clash with Ireland a week later in Dublin, but the English had a couple of surprises waiting for an All Blacks team that was beginning to show the signs of a long and hard season.

The All Blacks found themselves down 15–0 after 25 minutes on a sodden Twickenham turf. It had been raining all week in London, and the conditions (as well as the low expectations) suited the English just perfectly. After McKenzie pulled a try back, Beauden knew the time was right to exercise a bit of free licence to show that, if needed, he could split the uprights any time he liked. Despite the driving rain, Beauden called for a pass from the ruck around 30 metres out. His drop kick sailed straight through the sticks, and was a vital score in a game that ended 16–15 to the All Blacks. In all fairness, the result probably did the English more good than the All Blacks; many had predicted a much greater scoreline and it meant that their coach Eddie Jones' job was safe through to the World Cup.

Just to prove a point, Beauden kicked another one the next weekend in Dublin. In fact, he scored all the All Blacks' points in that game—which they lost 16–9. Beauden, Scott and a number of others could add the unwanted tag of being the first All Blacks to lose to Ireland twice, alongside being the first ones to do it at all.

Following a week of inquisition by the media travelling with the team and back home, it was almost a relief that the season would be over after what would prove to be an easy win in Rome against Italy. Jordie found himself back in the team, starting on the right wing. It marked the first time that all three brothers were in the starting line-up, and they'd make sure that dad Smiley, who had travelled to watch the boys play, would have something to brag about.

Like Beauden earlier in the year, Jordie had bounced back from the critics to score four tries in a match. They are the only two brothers to have achieved that feat in test rugby.

Jordie scored his first try after 31 minutes, running in a pass from McKenzie. He got his second after the half-time hooter went, leaping high to catch a cross-kick from Beauden's right boot. The next was off a kick too, but it came from the unlikely source of replacement hooker Nathan Harris in the seventy-fourth minute. Then, again after the hooter had gone to end the game, he strolled in off a Mo'unga pass to score in the corner. Just to put a cherry on top of the Barrett family day out, Beauden grabbed a try too. Almost fittingly, Scott put in a hard shift in the second row and never got anywhere close to scoring.

Like Beauden earlier in the year, Jordie had bounced back from the critics to score four tries in a match. They are the only two brothers to have achieved that feat in test rugby.

The Barrett name will be synonymous with All Blacks rugby

forever, but looking towards the future it may not be the most prominent brother who ends up playing the most tests. Scott, so often relied upon to be the workhorse, is in line to play a leading role from now on. He will be a key man for the All Blacks in the cycle leading up to the 2023 World Cup. Beauden's career is being given the Dan Carter clause, allowed to take a year to cash up in Japan after the 2019 World Cup. Jordie has several years before he hits the All Blacks wing expiry date like Julian Savea.

The Barretts currently have 111 tests between them (as of the start of the 2019 season). They still have a way to go to catch up with the Franks, Brooke and Whetton brothers, but the advantage of having one extra means that they will eventually most likely surpass and hold on to the record of most test caps by one family.

The Barretts have a special affinity with Ireland. They spent time there as kids, and Beauden and Scott both played their debuts against Ireland with differing fortunes. Jordie had his break against the British & Irish Lions. It's highly likely, given the Irish rise to prominence in the rugby world over the last few years, that a few more stories of the battles the brothers will have with them are yet to be written.

They are part of the tradition of family ties in the All Blacks. Like all rugby teams, it is a family in itself. Every time they step on the field, they are surrounded by a legacy of brotherhood.

ACKNOWLEDGEMENTS

Special thanks to Stephen Berg and his colleagues at the New Zealand Rugby Museum in Palmerston North, whose help was invaluable in researching this project. Thanks also to the team at Allen & Unwin for their hard work making it happen, and to Lynn McConnell for his helpful advice and encouragement.

I owe a special debt of gratitude to the people that set me on the path to achieving this effort: Marcus Stickley, Alex van Wel and Megan Whelan from RNZ (Radio New Zealand), Duncan Grieve, Mad Chapman and everyone at *The Spinoff*, Hone Edwards at Māori Television, Matt McCarthy at Rugby Wrap Up New York, and the many others who have given me a break over the years.

REFERENCES

Akers, Clive (2016), *Balls, Bullets and Boots.* Palmerston North: New Zealand Rugby Museum.

Allblacks.com

Brooke, Zinzan, with Alex Veysey (1995), *Zinny: The Zinzan Brooke Story.* Auckland: Rugby Publishing.

Clarke, Don, and Pat Booth (1966), *The Boot: Don Clarke's Story.* Wellington: A. H. & A. W. Reed.

Haden, Andy (1988), *Lock, Stock 'n Barrel.* Auckland: Rugby Press.

Hutchins, Graham (2006), *All Black Brothers.* Wellington: Grantham House.

Lewis, Paul (1991), *Brothers in Arms: The Alan & Gary Whetton Story.* Auckland: Moa.

Nepia, George, and Terry McLean (1963), *I, George Nepia: The Golden Years of Rugby Football.* Wellington: A. H. & A. W. Reed.

NZ Rugby Almanacks, 1940s to present.

Palenski, Ron, Rod Chester and Neville McMillan (2006, 7th revised edn), *Men in Black.* Auckland: Hachette New Zealand.

Ryan, Greg (1993), *Forerunners of the All Blacks: The 1888–89 New Zealand Native Football Team in Britain, Australia and New Zealand.* Christchurch: Canterbury University Press.

Turner, Brian (2002), *Meads.* Auckland: Hachette New Zealand.

NOTE: Throughout this book, the governing body of rugby in New Zealand is referred to as it was known at the time: the New Zealand Rugby Football Union (NZRFU) from 1892 to 2006, the New Zealand Rugby Union (NZRU) from 2006 to 2013, and New Zealand Rugby (NZR) from 2013 onwards.